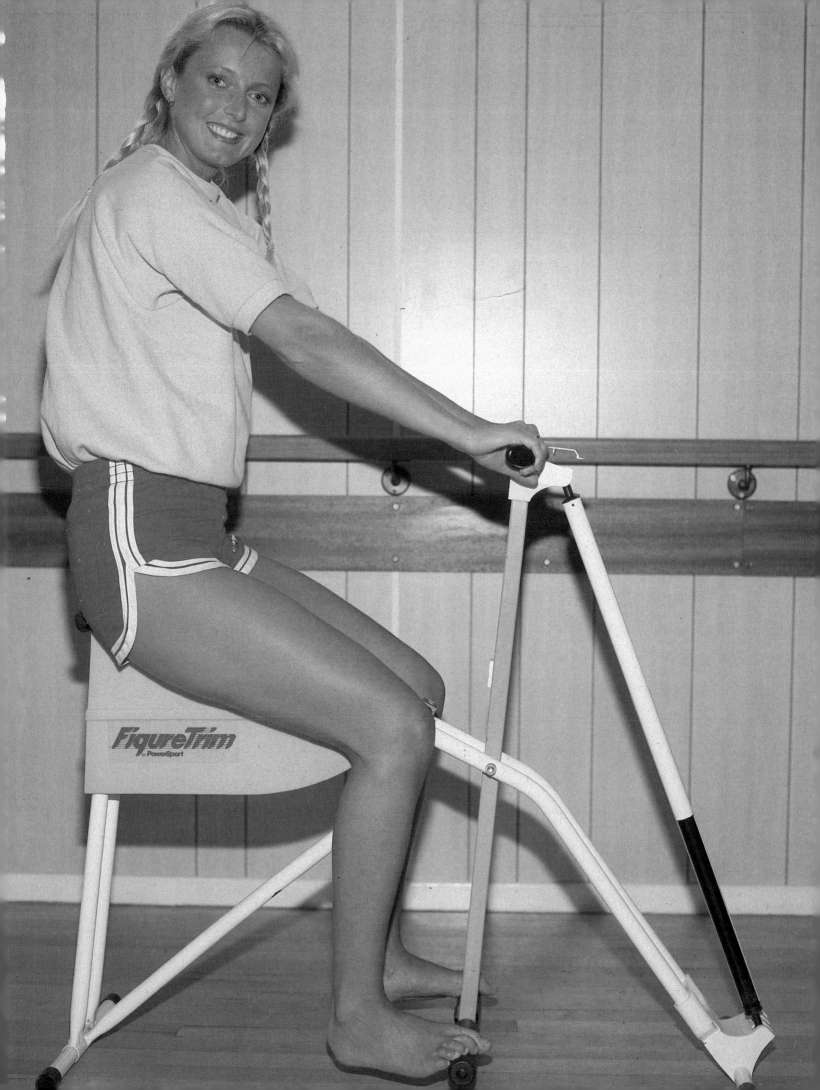

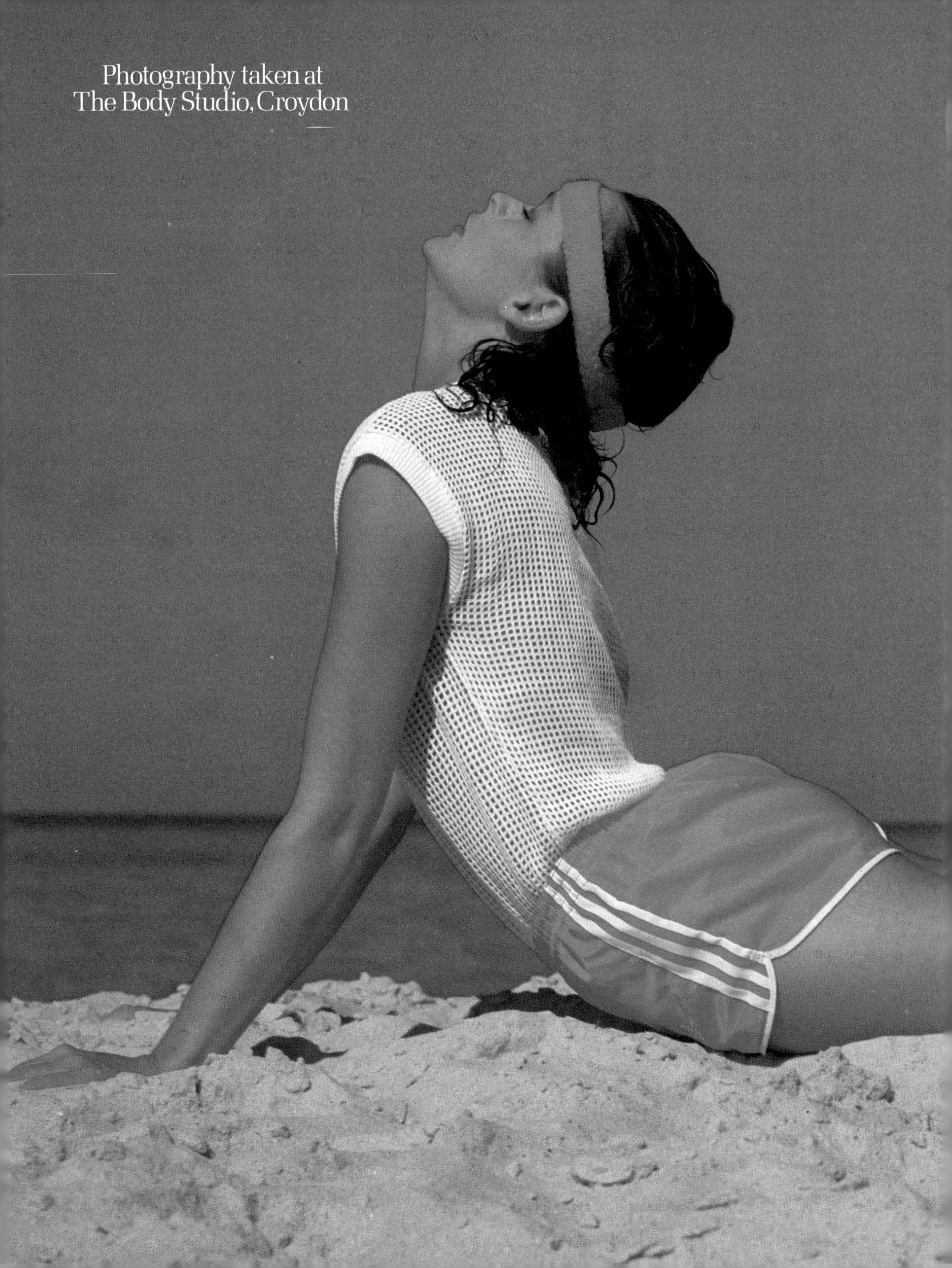

Photography taken at
The Body Studio, Croydon

SHAPE UP AND FEEL GREAT

Ann Carpenter

Technical Adviser
Helene Johnson

DESIGNED BY
Philip Clucas MSIAD

PHOTOGRAPHY BY
Peter Barry

PRODUCED BY
Ted Smart & David Gibbon

GREENWICH HOUSE

Why WorkOut?

Creator of the exercise programmes for 'The Complete Workout Book': Helene Johnson.

To improve the entire quality of your life, that's why. An extravagant boast? Not in the least. A well-planned, sensible and regular lifetime programme of exercise will help you feel better, look better and enable you to enjoy a much fuller life than you may have been leading until now.

Exercise will not make you lose weight but it will burn up calories, firm muscles and re-distribute inches. Regular exercise performed alongside a sensible, wholesome, calorie-controlled diet will make weight loss quicker and easier and will eventually result in an *improved* silhouette.

Working your body in a controlled manner means more oxygen is delivered to the tissues, circulation improves, banishing feelings of sluggishness and joints are loosened up making even daily movement more of a fundamental pleasure.

Exercise will enliven and awaken the whole system making you feel less tired and more alert. It will keep the body in good working order, enabling it to run more efficiently, helping it combat common ailments.

Medical research has concluded that it can help prevent heart disease, cure back pain, encourage efficiently working heart muscles, lungs and respiratory system and act as a powerful force in reducing tension and stress. New mothers will also testify to the beneficial effect regular exercises have on childbirth and regaining the figure afterwards.

Get Exercise On Your Side

For many people – men, women and children alike – the scourge of modern living is stress. Stress can initiate a whole host of physical disorders: headaches, migraine, digestive disorders, back trouble, tension in the neck and shoulders and skin complaints, to name just a few.

Think how most of us automatically cope with stress. We have a good stretch. This in itself is a fundamental, instinctive exercise. It irons out the back, neck and arms, enabling the system to have a 'breather'.

Exercise fights this arch enemy of health and happiness. It is free and it only takes ten minutes each day or two or three hours a week to do. So, when stress strikes out at *you*, before dashing to the doctor for a prescription for tranquillisers, sleeping pills or laxatives, consider tackling these problems from another angle. If these ailments aren't yet acute, embark on some form of regular exercise – even if it's only a brisk, 15-minute walk each day.

With evidence as strong as this to contemplate, it's easy to see why so many people are now making working-out an integral part of their lives. But getting started can sometimes prove a problem.

Getting Started

We all have gravity to contend with and are being constantly pulled earthward. It is therefore tempting to spend life in a perpetual slouch. The comfortable pose of the sloth is an easy one to fall into and the more we do it, the more habitual it becomes. This makes drawing ourselves up to our full height to embark on some kind of working-out routine all the harder.

But imagine what years of slouching and lack of free, mobile movement can do to the body. Think of all those vital organs being compressed into cramped positions, unable to do the job they were designed for at maximum efficiency. Picture the long-suffering spine distorted into a perpetual curve and consider how it will gradually 'set' into this position as we pass through middle and into old age. But old age doesn't *have* to mean slack muscles and shrunken, stooping bodies.

One Good Body

Most of us were born with one good body that is expected to function efficiently for seventy years or more. Each and every day of our lives it will be working away performing hundreds of tasks we either have no knowledge of or have come to take for granted.

Only at night, when we are sleeping, does it have the opportunity to rebuild and 'service' all those vital parts. Most people would agree that this is no mean task. Surely the least we can do is assist our body in its work by taking far greater care of it. Just improving posture is one small step in the right direction.

Think Positive

It's amazing how many reasons we can conjure up for not keeping healthy, happy and FIT. "Oh I can't possibly spend 15 minutes a day working-out. After all, there's the housework/shopping/professional job to do, then there's the garage to clear out and all those shelves to put up in the sitting room. Then I've got to get dinner, do the ironing and the children are *constantly* demanding. And I simply *must* file my nails! And, after all that, I only have the energy to flop in front of the T.V." These excuses are all too familiar.

If you want to dedicate your life to becoming a fat, flabby, unattractive slob, lacking in mental and physical vitality, fine. Slump back and deteriorate – no one will force you to do otherwise. But this book is obviously not for you.

However, if you want more energy, a firmer body, a brighter mind, a more satisfactory sex life, a more optimistic outlook on life in general and are prepared to *make* time for exercising, then think positively and read on. Working-out can do all this for you and probably a whole lot more.

Fitting an exercise routine into your life each day or a couple of times a week will lessen the burden of the rest of your chores. It will help you cope better with your job and even the housework. Clearing out the garage will become less of a daunting task. And the kids – well, take them exercising with you. It will not only keep them occupied but they'll have a new horizon in their lives, too.

Exercise is not a Drudge

Working-out should not be a daily chore, it should become a lifetime habit.

Considering then, how beneficial exercise can be, how little it costs both in terms of money and time, why is it so many people wilt at the thought of even walking to the off licence when they can easily cover that 200 yards in the car? Why do they pale at the idea of taking the dog round the block when there's a 'perfectly good back garden' outside?

Unfortunately exercise had got a bad name for itself. Sad but true. Much of the blame must lie with the media, the rest with bad exercise teachers and those infuriating 'holier than thou' exercise fanatics.

"Exercise only works if it's painful and exhausting" is a ridiculous myth that, unfortunately, has established itself as a credible fact. Articles in magazines and books have, in the past, directed us to force limbs into unnatural positions and hold them there, with no consideration for our age or state of fitness.

Some exercise teachers assume *all* their students will be able to tackle *all* exercises and occasionally take the foolish line of pushing people beyond their natural capabilities. They build up a sense of competition in the class, cruelly ridiculing those who lag behind. This kind of class is fine for masochists but not for the rest. It can cause permanent physical damage to untrained, unfit bodies.

Fitness fanatics are never happy unless they are running on the spot. Lean as a reed, perpetually dressed in a tracksuit or pair of shorts, they talk ceaselessly about their cardio-vascular system, bore everyone rigid relating their latest feats of stamina and physical endurance. They rarely miss the opportunity to point out how much fitter and better *their* bodies are in comparison to *yours*.

Mental Determination

All these facts combine to put the person who doesn't exercise right off the whole idea.

But working-out – to some degree – is for everyone, be they young, old or even physically handicapped. Of course it takes a degree of effort and some discomfort is to be expected. After a thorough work-out, bodies that are used to immobility will certainly ache.

Any exercise routine requires a certain amount of mental determination and physical exertion. Sweating and breathlessness are likely to occur. But the wave of relief your body experiences while being thoroughly stretched and refreshed and the increasing feeling of energy and sense of well-being that is achieved will make a few aches and pains totally worthwhile.

Fitness is Fun

Exercise means treating your body with new respect, working with it instead of against it. And all this should be fun. It is therefore important to select a method that suits you and your personality. After all, despite the vast numbers of people who apply to enter the Marathons each year, not everyone is a born jogger.

The will to work at exercise stems from a genuine desire to take part in it. This desire manifests itself only if you have selected the type of exercise that you feel happy doing. Some people thrive on the competitive kind of exercise found with tennis or squash. Others prefer the non-competitive varieties such as walking and yoga. Many people like to push themselves as far as their bodies will allow them; others only enjoy exercise if they can incorporate it into their lives at a more steady pace. We are all different personalities and it would be ridiculous to assume that we will all enjoy the same kinds of work-outs.

Exercise means running, walking, rowing, swimming and cycling. It means joining an evening class and doing Keep Fit, following the slower but deep and far reaching postures of yoga, bashing a ball around a tennis court twice a week, donning a bright pink leotard and leg warmers and 'tuning-in' to aerobics or dancing around a church hall, along with a couple of dozen others in a dance movement routine. It means spending 10 minutes a day doing some deep breathing and a few simple postures. Exercises come in all forms and guises. In order to enjoy them to the full, find the method that your mind and body feels most at home with. Don't let it become a chore or an obsession. If you have to miss your weekly or daily routine, then don't panic. Just return to your programme when you can.

The Complete Work Out Book is a comprehensive guide to exercise covering all its many aspects. It is designed with all kinds of people in mind–and not just the already sylph-like few. It explores the most fundamental rules of sensible exercise– posture and relaxation. It is a complete programme for a whole new kind of fitness and well being.

The core of *Complete Work Out Book* is a specially developed programme of exercises that you can do, yourself, at home. This programme leaves no part of the body un-tuned. As well as exercises for things like tummy muscles and thighs, there are ones for your neck and shoulders and even your hands and feet. A worthwhile, sensible exercise programme takes all parts of the body into consideration. Each and every part of us is vital to our daily lives and requires equal care and attention.

In order to appeal to all ages, we have exercises for the fit and supple and ones for beginners, too.

There are long routines for the dedicated, quicker ones of the hopelessly busy. These routines have been produced to work as the only exercise plan you will ever need, or they can be used in conjunction with another kind of method such as cycling or walking.

The Best of Both Worlds

Since many people like to work-out in groups, under the supervision of a trained teacher, we have included sections on other, established methods, explaining how they work.

With this, you have the best of both worlds: a fully-comprehensive exercise plan to do at home in harmony with a class for a specific method.

There is little point in working-out if you have severe posture faults. Otherwise you will just be working on these faults and eventually accentuating them. For this reason we show you how to align your body correctly before embarking on our programme. Many people refuse to consider their posture as an important factor in their general health. But good, correct posture is a mighty powerful force.

As well as this there are sections on pregnancy, yoga, weight training and exercising in the water.

Follow our programme carefully and with regularity and see how your mental outlook as well as your body changes. Don't expect miracles after only a few weeks. Good, worthwhile, exercise can mean a lifetime of dedication. The results will eventually manifest themselves in the smooth functioning of your body as a whole– mind and limbs alike.

So what are you waiting for? Read on…work-out…and start living!

In the Beginning

Good exercise means first learning about good posture.

There is a growing feeling among exercise teachers and those who have closely studied the workings of the body, that posture plays a far more vital role in our general well-being than we once thought. But these days, correct posture means far more than walking in a straight line balancing several hefty books on your head without dropping them. This is the old-fashioned idea of how to succeed in walking with elegant grace.

In reality, there is little point in standing rigidly erect and looking elegant and graceful if your bones, joints and muscles aren't correctly aligned in the first place. Posture means a whole lot more than how you hold yourself when standing around at a cocktail party.

The Big Slump

These days, most of us can rarely incorporate sufficient bodily movement in our daily lives. Tilling the land in order to earn our daily bread is a task of the past. Instead, in the modern world, most of us spend eight hours a day sitting hunched in an office, driving around in a car, perpetually bent double to attend small children or turning knobs and buttons in order to operate some kind of automated machinery. Because we are now geared to labour saving devices – both at work and in the home, this means our bodies do far less physical work.

The result is that we spend a vast amount of our waking hours slumped in one kind of sedentary position or another. How are you sitting as you are reading this book? Don't move, just run over the various parts of your body and picture how they are aligned. Possibly your shoulders are rounded, your spine slumped in a forwards or sideways curve.

Whether sitting, standing or lying down, we develop and adopt postural habits as we mature. Then as we grow old, these habits become accentuated. Finally, they become so 'set' into round, stooping shoulders and curved spines, it is impossible to attempt to rectify them.

Do You Know How to Stand?

It is extraordinary how the most commonplace stances in life can lead to complete lack of correct body alignment. Take shoulder bags, for example. These have been fashionable for women for a number of years and most women will, quite unconsciously, carry their heavy bag over the *same* shoulder every time they go out. Now consider just how this one action can throw your entire body out of alignment. Say you always throw your bag over the left shoulder – this is automatically pulled down which means the right shoulder is forced *up*. The spine is slightly curved to follow the dictates of the shoulders and this, in turn, leads to the hips and pelvic area being thrown out of alignment. It's fascinating to consider how one small, seemingly insignificant movement can cause such disruption everywhere else. One way to rectify the situation would be to

alternate your shoulders when carrying the bag!

Many of us are used to adopting a specific kind of pose when we are standing around or talking to people. One of the most common poses is to stand with arms folded across the chest, one leg straight and the other knee slightly bent. Again, the shoulders slope down towards one side, the pelvis is at an angle and one thigh is forced into the hip area while the other stretches out towards the bent knee.

The same faults can be spotted when sitting down. Most of us have a favourite pose we adopt when watching television or are curled up in an armchair reading a book or newspaper. Sitting postures take many forms but most are likely to mean stress is placed on one side of the body for most of the time. Just taking stock of the way you usually sit, then carefully going over the entire body when you are in this stance will give you some idea of how your body is shaped most of the time.

By first understanding this, then acting on it – even moving around so you aren't in the same position all the time – will ensure your body has a better chance of correctly functioning for the rest of your life.

Don't Accentuate Your Body Faults

It is not easy to re-educate the body into correct posture. For a start, we are working against the laws of gravity, which keep pulling us earthward and makes straightening-up that much more of a chore. But a little practice every day will gradually turn into a habit and your body will feel *more* comfortable in the correct postural position than it did before.

But good posture is not only of prime importance in everyday actions, it also has a tremendously powerful bearing on the results of an exercise method. If your body is out of alignment before you embark on a programme, you will simply be working on your alignment faults and, eventually accentuating them.

A really knowledgable and caring exercise teacher will inform his or her students about the correct way to position the body before attempting to take up a particular exercise. Good body alignment can work *for* you when you are exercising. It can actually make the exercises easier in some cases, whereas bad posture can make them much more difficult to achieve.

Learn to Relax in a Pose

I have attended exercise classes of many different kinds over the past couple of years and one of the things I have noticed particularly is the way people make poses more difficult for themselves than they need be. Naturally there is bound to be a certain amount of effort and discomfort when you are pushing the body into a stance it is not normally accustomed to adopting. But there is a marked difference between strain and effort. Effort works *for* the body, enabling it to reap as much benefit as possible from a pose. Strain serves only to work against it – and probably won't be doing that much good in the long run as a result.

Teachers of yoga advocate *relaxing* into a pose and I think there's a lot of good sense in this. Relaxing into a pose means getting your shoulders, spine, back, hips, legs and arms in the right places *before* you attempt to hold the position. It then means adopting the final pose and feeling happy and comfortable there. When all these parts of the body are in the wrong places, the students will suffer. They will strain in all the wrong places, get out of breath and find the whole exercise an extremely difficult one to execute.

At a good exercise class, the teacher will pay careful attention to the individual students and constantly correct postural faults. The Iyengar method of yoga, in particular, pays great attention to how the feet are positioned before attempting the various postures (note how they call the exercises 'postures').

Take the Triangle posture. You stand with your feet two and a half feet apart, slightly turning to the right and slowly bend the trunk down to the right side keeping one hand on your ankle for support. The head and chest are turned to face the ceiling and the free arm is raised vertically. Before you start, your feet should be in exactly the right position with toes firmly spread out for a good grip on the ground. This provides a firm, solid base for what is to follow. Feet that are badly positioned could mean you stretch too far forward or back. Elementary postural faults such as this, which may seem insignificant, can completely negate the benefits of the whole exercise. If you are not sitting, lying or standing properly when you are doing an exercise then you may as well not bother for all the good it will do you.

How to Stand and Sit Correctly

A very common postural fault is to stand in what you *think* is a straight, erect position with bottom pushed out, the spine curving inwards and the abdomen thrust slightly forwards. In reality it means strain in the lower spine with weight being thrown into the pelvic area.

Here is how to stand in the correct way with the body satisfactorily aligned: place the feet hip-width apart, turn them slightly out and check your weight is evenly distributed over the feet for correct balance. Now spread your toes as far apart as you can. Try and feel the floor beneath you. It will give you some idea of the strength and importance of feet when it comes to maintaining good balance.

Now see how your pelvis feels when it is tilted in various directions. Placing your hands either side of your waist, tilt your pelvis forwards as far as it will go and feel the buttocks tightening, the thighs straining. Now tilt it back and up so your bottom raises and your spine curves inwards. Both these positions are exaggerated but will give you a practical and highly effective demonstration of how the way you align your pelvis determines the position of the rest of your body. The right way is to tilt it slightly up in front so the back and bottom are in a straighter line. Your lower spine will automatically lengthen and your abdomen tighten. Your bottom will also tighten and your thighs and knees turn outwards.

Lift Off From the Crown

Now go to the top of your head. Make sure it is central – not too far forward or back – and imagine it is being lifted up from the crown. Let the chin drop forwards very slightly. These actions will cause your back to straighten up even more. Relax your shoulders downwards with arms hanging loosely beside the hips. Both these head and shoulder positions will automatically cause your neck to lengthen. In this final position, your ribs are lifted slightly and expanded for more efficient, unrestricted breathing.

One of the most common *wrong* ways to sit is with shoulders slumped forwards. This causes the chin to jut out which in turn compresses the back of the neck and shoulders, possibly leading to tension if you sit in this manner for a long time. Shoulders hunched deep into the neck also serve to restrict the flow of blood to the head. If all this sounds complicated, try it for yourself and see.

The *right* way to sit is with your feet positioned hip-wide apart on the floor and turning out slightly. Thighs are also hip-wide apart (it's difficult to sit with your knees knocking together however dignified we have been led to believe this looks!) and knees are placed at almost a right angle to the torso, in front. Again, position your pelvis so it is tilting very slightly up at the front. This will automatically cause the lower spine to lengthen – and help alleviate any tension in that area.

Imagine the head being comfortably drawn up from the crown while gently relaxing your shoulders downwards. Through this action, the neck lengthens at the back. Finally, in the completed position, the ribs will be lifted, enabling deeper, more relaxed breathing, there will be more length in the torso and the abdomen will be drawn inwards but not cramped. Sitting like this will free the rib area for more efficient breathing and the whole abdomen and digestive area will be opened-up rather than compressed, which only leads to an impaired digestive system.

Make Good Posture a Habit

If all these directions sound complicated and time-consuming and far too much trouble to put into daily practice, just try them once, running through your body and judging exactly how each part of it feels when correctly aligned. The end result is so natural and comfortable you'll feel for yourself how much sense it makes to adopt this stance whenever possible. Obviously you won't be able to stand and sit in this manner always. But when you are standing and sitting in a particularly angular, slumped or balled-up position, try returning to the correct way of alignment and gradually it will become a habit.

Now that you have some idea of how the body should feel when all the joints, muscles and bones are in their rightful place, you can start on the exercises from a strong, healthy and positive position.

10-Minute Posture and Relaxation Plan

One excellent exercise teacher I know is called Barbara Dale, who runs her own exercise classes called the Bodyworkshop at the Lambton Squash Club, London W11. In particular, Barbara has made a careful study of the way we hold ourselves, and much of her wisdom and knowledge has been incorporated in this chapter. Barbara believes in exercising with care and respect for your body at all times. She advocates working up to vigorous exercises slowly

and understanding the importance of relaxation.

Barbara has devised a special pick-up plan which takes only about ten minutes and can be performed before exercises to prepare the body for movement and, afterwards, to relax it. This plan incorporates correct body alignment when lying down–as well as acting as a powerful relaxing therapy for tired bodies and minds.

1. Lie flat on the floor with a mat or towel underneath you for comfort. Gently ease yourself into the floor rather than just 'flaking-out'. Now straighten your body by checking that your chin is in line with your pubic bone. Your arms should lie loosely down to the side and knees should be several inches apart, rolling out.

2. In order to relax your back further, press down using your head and elbows for support, so your back and chest are lifted up and off the floor. Let your back go down to the floor again, trying to work the back of your waist flat on the floor.

3. Lifting your head, tilt your chin slightly forward in order to give a slight stretch to the back of the neck. Now drop your head back again and roll it from side to side to loosen the neck.

4. With your arms down to the sides, pull your shoulders down towards the hands, away from the head.

5. Your arms should be resting several inches from the sides of your

body with palms facing upwards. No contact with the floor means hands and fingers can relax further. If your hands automatically clench when they face up, place the palms downwards or just rest them either side of your abdomen.

6. To further relax the back, bend your knees slightly and press the back of the waist into the floor. At the same time, tilt your pelvis upwards then relax down.

7. Now straighten your legs again, with your knees slightly apart and rolling out, then shake your legs to loosen them.

8. Turn both your feet in a clockwise direction and repeat the other way. Try to push your toes down to the carpet in front and bring them back again to right-angles with the legs. Wriggle your toes about and relax your feet, letting them fall outwards.

9. Now take two or three deep breaths expanding the abdomen as you breathe in and contracting it as you breathe out again. Next, breathe in, expanding the abdomen and try to breathe in still further, expanding the chest. Do this just once.

10. You should now be feeling very relaxed and comfortable, but to calm your mind still further, either concentrate on your breathing pattern for a couple of minutes or try to conjure up nice memories of sun, sea and sand. Don't worry if your mind wanders to another subject or to your daily worries. If it does, then gently take it back to the good memory once more.

Body Types

We are all cast in different moulds and must learn to like what we've got.

Body types are just as much subject to the whims of fashion as haircuts and hemlines. But the trouble with our bodies is, although they can lose excess fat or build up muscle, they can't be altered with the same extreme, ruthless abandon that top Paris designers transform silhouettes from one season to the next.

Obviously it is ludicrous to suggest that if, for example, very thin, straight-up-and-down bodies are upheld as the 'high fashion' shape of one decade, then the other ninety percent of the population, whose figures don't conform to this 'ideal', are to be written off as undesirable. Instead, we must come to terms with what our figure type is, learn how to make the most of it but, most important of all, come to like the way we look. Chances are, if we are happy with our physiques, then our confidence will be projected to others.

We have only to consider such successful and charismatic people as Woody Allen, Bette Midler, Dolly Parton and Dudley Moore to realise that even if our looks don't conform to the currently fashionable ideal, we can still become sex symbols!

The Ever Changing Ideal

Looking at all the different figure types that have, over the ages, been upheld as the most desirable forms, it seems ridiculous even to attempt to emulate.

Many of the great, classical painters and sculptors chose to create likenesses of women that would, today, be described as frankly obese. Full, pear-shaped hips encompassing ample, fleshy thighs were 'quite the thing' in those days. Bosoms were positively tiny by comparison.

The pre-Raphaelite painters favoured slender, waif-like figures under faces that were fine-boned, delicate and perpetually wistful looking. In the Edwardian era, the desirable figure was a full bosom over a tiny waist that perched above generous, shapely hips – the ultimate 'hour glass' figure. Fashionable women of the twenties cut their hair into boyish crops and strived to make their bodies look equally boyish by strapping down their breasts and wearing slim, tubular frocks that allowed no suggestion of a waistline.

Coming on Strong

The big, Hollywood screen characters of the forties were assertive women of strong and independent character. Actresses such as Barbara Stanwyck, Joan Crawford and Ingrid Bergman filled these roles admirably. The robust, natural good looks of Ingrid Bergman were revolutionary at the time and, at first, Hollywood studios were all for moulding her into the traditional, glamorous, film star image that was then acceptable. But Ingrid Berman, being the strong-willed, confident character that she was in real life, refused to let them tamper with her own distinctive beauty (a prime example of self-confidence). The result was she became one of the most successful actresses of the following decades. Joan Crawford and

Barbara Stanwyck introduced their own brand of self-assurance into the characters they portrayed and their bodies projected this power and confidence with the help of fashion: broad shouldered dresses and suits were given an assertive boost by the addition of some hefty shoulder padding.

In the fifties, shapely, well-covered bodies were back in vogue once more. Actresses such as Shelly Winters, Jane Russell, Marilyn Monroe, Kim Novak and Jayne Mansfield filled their roles (literally!) with great gusto.

The Thin Revolution

The sixties proved to be a decade of revolution in a myriad different ways. The meteoric rise to fame of such people as photographers David Bailey and Terence Donovan, actors such as Terence Stamp and the most famous crimper of them all, Vidal Sassoon, meant you didn't *have* to be born with a silver spoon in your mouth in order to be successful in life. In fact, it was a real boost to your charismatic appeal if you were born in the East End of London and left secondary modern school at the age of 15.

In the sixties Britain ruled the waves of fashion and where they trod their stylishly booted toes, the rest of the world followed. In music, clothes, hairstyles, with a great enthusiasm for breaking all the rules of convention that had preceded them, the British explored and fulfilled their potential for being the most eccentric people in the modern Western world.

During this time of inventiveness and revolution a brand new physique ideal evolved. Suddenly THIN was IN. The opportunity presented itself for waif-like, almost totally flat chested women to rejoice in and flaunt their unconventionally lovely, gamine bodies. And exploit them they did, to the hilt, in what was to become the most fashionable career for a young woman to dabble in – the world of professional fashion modelling.

The extraordinarily beautiful, gazelle-like Jean Shrimpton emerged at the beginning of the decade to become one of the most photographed women in the world. Then, in the middle sixties, a young girl heralding from the unprepossessing London suburb of Neasden, completely revolutionised the way women were to look for years to come. Lesley Hornby, a spaghetti-thin 16 year-old, adopted the new name of Twiggy and, overnight, a whole new look in fashion was born. The Daily Express devoted a whole page to her, labelled her 'The Face of '66' – and she was.

In weeks, Twiggy became a cult. She had her photograph on the cover of Paris Match magazine, put her name to a range of clothes, launched a collection of clothes-brush style false eyelashes. By 1968 it wasn't enough to be slim anymore. You had to be positively *thin*.

The success of Twiggy's look was, in a way, encouraging. It proved that if you had confidence in what may be an unconventional brand of looks, and the guts to promote them, not only could you be accepted by the whole world, but the whole world would want to look like you too.

Unfortunately, the success of Twiggy and the other reed-slender models and actresses of the sixties who cultivated similar physiques, gave birth to a mania for dieting that is still obsessing vast numbers of women today. Book shops groan under the weight of new publications telling women how to become thin. A new diet seems to emerge every month and 'slimming' publications constantly top the best-selling lists. We seem addicted to losing flesh.

The trouble with many diets is that they do anything but promote healthy, sensible, well-balanced, unobsessive eating.

Healthy Not Thin

But happily things are beginning to change. For a start, it is no longer fashionable to be *thin*. The desirable body of today is much more well-covered than it was back in the sixties. It is also fashionable to look healthy, and looking healthy does not mean boasting legs and thighs with the girth of asparagus sticks.

With such an emphasis on eating for health, level-headed people now understand the importance of wholefoods such as brown rice, wholemeal bread and pulses – all foods which were 'outlawed' by the diet-obsessed a decade ago. Even the nutritional value of potatoes cooked in their skins is now being understood. It isn't the poor old potato that piles on the inches, it's the butter and fat it's often prepared in that does the damage.

These days, the modern, liberated woman is less susceptible to conforming to a 'type' that may be deemed fashionable by the media or promoted in advertising campaigns. She is much more concerned with taking stock of what nature endowed her with and learning how to make the best of her body than trying to alter it completely to suit someone else's fantasy. Modern women are now eating for inner health and not just to be skinny.

The Three Body Types

Fashion aside, body types have been categorised into three basic groups.

Ectomorphs are the slender people of the world. They are also inclined to be on the tall side. Some of them are extremely thin and lanky and never seem to gain an ounce of fat however much they eat. As well as finding it difficult to accumulate fat, they often find it equally hard to develop their muscles.

Mesomorphs are strong, strapping types, sturdily built and naturally physically powerful. They find it quite easy to build muscle and will excel in sports that require strength such as weight lifting. Rugger players with their burly shoulders and well-developed limbs could be classified as typical mesomorphs. Without regular work-outs, however, their strong physiques can run to flab.

Endomorphs are the ones who will have to watch their food intake and make regular exercise a part of their daily programme if they are not to become overweight. They are sturdily built – sometimes stout and well-covered with flesh – although by no means necessarily fat. A typical endomorph would be a stocky, hockey-playing or shot-putting type.

Body Construction

Your body type will have a marked bearing on the kind of exercise you are likely to do well at – or find heavy going. Well-built muscular sorts are naturals for body-building contests and short-distance running. They are less likely to excel at long-distance, endurance events. Swimmers have powerful shoulders and arms and are well-covered with flesh. Runners and hurdlers have lean, long-limbed physiques.

But even if we aren't professional sportspeople, the way our bodies are constructed still influences our ability to exercise.

One exercise method which highlights this perfectly is yoga. It is fascinating to see how the length of a person's neck, arms, torso or legs will determine the ease with which they carry out the various postures. Those with long arms will find the Spinal Twist much easier than people who have short arms. Men, who often have much more power in their arms and shoulders than women, lift their bodies into perfect headstands with the kind of ease that is disheartening to onlookers. It is quite usual for women to spend months – even years – getting their legs straight up into the air. Women, on the other hand, can accomplish any kind of forward bend much more easily than the men – who often have trouble just touching their toes! This obviously has a lot to do with the way women are constructed in the lower back and hip area.

The positive thing about understanding different body types is the knowledge that if you are hopeless at one kind of exercise or sport – you'll probably be terrific at another. This doesn't mean that you shouldn't *try* to do well at sports or exercises that don't come easily. It just means understanding your limitations – and discovering your true potential.

When the book has been read and understood you can start your programme, progressing from one star – 1-2 weeks – going on to two stars for a further 2-3 weeks depending on the programme or the individual ability. Progress onto the three star exercises by 5-6 weeks – this will be your maintenance level.

The Exercises

The Star Guides to the Exercises

The exercises in the 'Complete Workout Book' have been categorised whenever possible into:

★ **Easy**
★★ **Medium**
★★★ **Advanced**

This will enable you to see, at a glance, the degree of difficulty of each movement.

★ **Easy:** movements for beginners with very little exercise – always start with these first.

★★ **Medium:** movements designed with the intermediate person in mind – a natural progression from the easy stage.

★★★ **Advanced:** movements for the advanced person who has progressed successfully from the first two stages – these will maintain your fitness level (when they become too easy, increase your counts by double or more).

These star symbols are merely guides for people new to exercise who are not certain of their bodies' capability or potential.

Be sure to thoroughly read the written text before embarking on any of the exercise programmes.

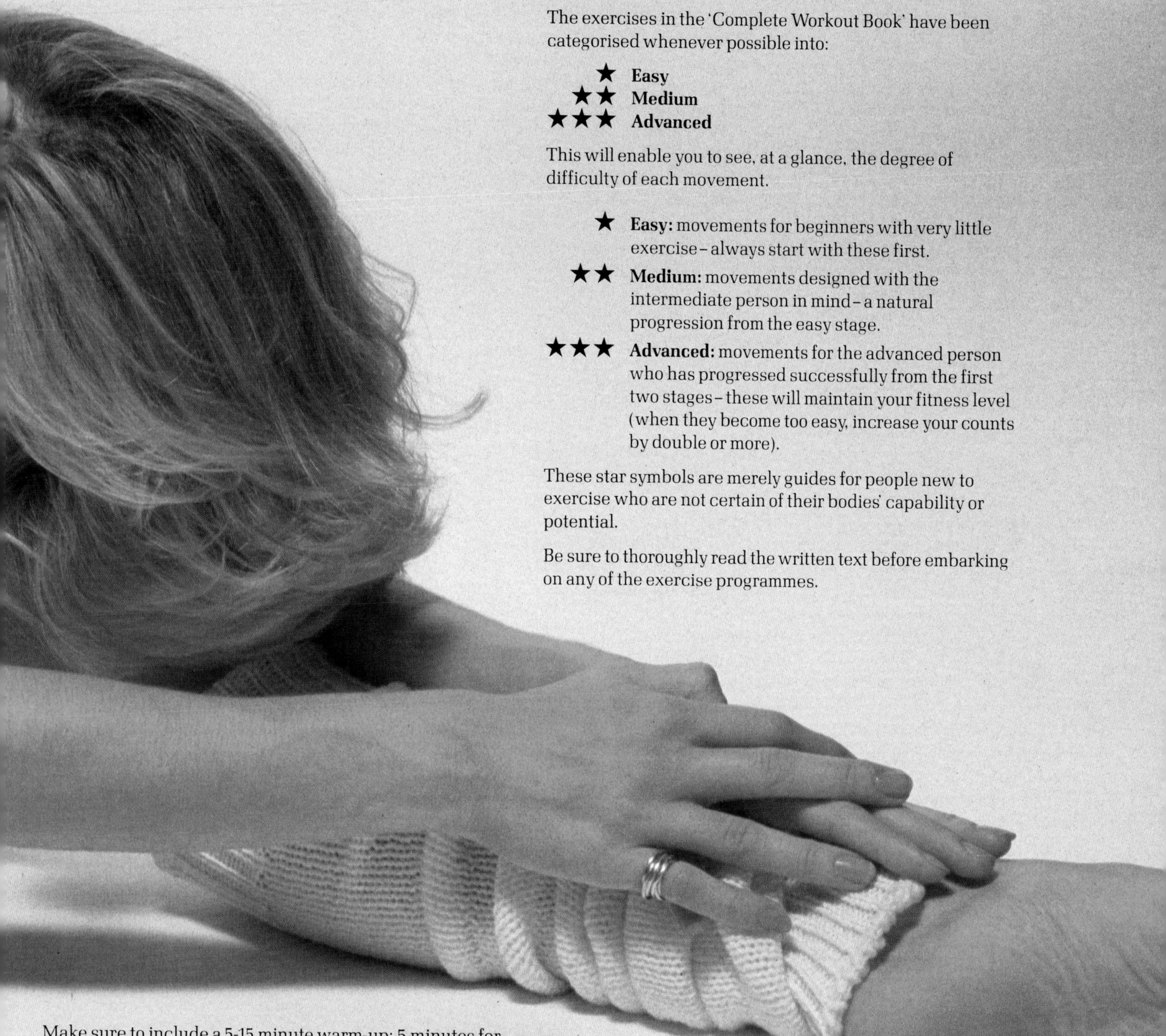

Make sure to include a 5-15 minute warm-up: 5 minutes for one star, 10minutes for two stars and 15 minutes for three stars.

Please listen to your body and your unique individual capabilities.

Aerobics

The word 'aerobic' is a fairly new and certainly fashionable one. But the kind of exercises it encompasses are nothing new at all.

The term 'aerobics' was originally coined by an American fitness expert called Dr Kenneth Cooper. The jogging craze which has swept both America and Britain is also thought to be directly traced to Dr Cooper's enthusiasm.

Aerobic exercise simply means exercising with air, or rather oxygen. It means exercising at a sustained speed and therefore increasing the body's demand – or more specifically, the demand of the heart and lungs – for oxygen. Muscles also need oxygen to function and, when we work them hard, their need increases dramatically. When we exercise in this way, we breathe more quickly and our pulse rate rises.

There are many different exercise methods which come under the aerobic umbrella. These include jogging, cycling, skipping, swimming and even walking very enthusiastically uphill.

These are all endurance exercises that increase the body's ability to deliver blood to the muscles and organs. It is the blood which bears the oxygen used to produce energy.

If you are very unfit, aerobic exercise should be embarked on with caution and built up to gradually. If you rush at it with great gusto and push yourself too hard, you will only exhaust yourself and feel so rotten afterwards you'll be put off forever.

Those who regularly practice aerobic exercise wax lyrical about the benefits. After regular, sensible practice, breathing will improve, the muscles of the chest and abdomen will obtain more vitality and the lungs will get more oxygen than they've been used to so their ability to clear out toxic waste will be increased.

The muscles of the body will strengthen and consequently endurance will improve. It is also said that metabolism is stimulated by aerobic activity. All in all, it must be concluded that anyone practicing a regular aerobic exercise programme that suits their bodies and their physical needs, will feel much better, fitter and healthier in the long run.

Aerobic exercise won't make you lose weight – although it will burn up calories. Effective weight loss can, however, be encouraged if these vigorous exercises are done regularly in conjunction with a sensible diet. Instead they will firm-up your muscles, improve your flexibility and, in some cases, alter the shape of your body by redistributing inches.

Don't Rush Headlong into Aerobics

As I mentioned before, most of us lead sedentary lives and are completely unused to any form of aerobic exercise. For this reason, the more vigorous varieties should be approached with caution. You benefit considerably if you plan some kind of warming-up routine before embarking on aerobics. And warming-up beforehand will make vigorous exercise easier to cope with.

A warming-up routine entails stretching and relaxing all parts of your body so that you feel refreshed but not exhausted afterwards. Have a look at the following warming-up routine illustrated here and select some exercises that suit you. A fair amount of common sense must be employed with these. For example, don't attempt anything that proves painful. Don't strive to achieve a posture that is clearly impossible for your untrained body to cope with. If the exercises are too hard for you, then use them as models on which to base simpler ones.

It is far more beneficial to do an exercise correctly to *some* degree rather than to attempt it fully and do it the wrong way. For example, let us look at exercises 1B and 1C in the 'Warming-up' section. Unless you are a classically trained dancer or have been doing yoga for a few years, it is highly unlikely you will be able to achieve the kind of flexibility our model is capable of. So with these exercises, instead of straining your body to bend your chest right down to the side of your knee, bend your knee and stretch your other leg out as far as it will comfortably go. Now bend your torso forwards so you are making slightly more effort than you are normally used to – but without risking actual physical damage!

If exercise 7 seems out of the question, just part your legs wide, keeping your knees tight and take one hand down to the knee. Twist your body as much as you can and try to take your other arm (keeping it straight) round to the back. Remember, you don't *have* to copy these exercises exactly in order to make them work for you. Providing it is approached with a degree of common sense, *any* exercise will be doing you good even if it isn't carried out as efficiently as the experts demonstrate.

Listen to Your Body

Remember, your own body probably has a far better idea of its capabilities than your mental expectations or a teacher who pushes the class too hard. For this reason, listen to what your body is telling you at all times. And if it shouts 'Stop!', then do so.

I have attended several different kinds of exercise classes which have required the students (many of whom seemed extremely unfit) to push their limbs and bodies into highly alien positions. At these classes, no allowances have been made for the fact that students were at considerably varying stages of fitness and suppleness. For those who found the exercise very difficult to achieve, the effects were negative rather than positive. If you find an exercise particularly awkward and hard to execute, you are likely to be straining the wrong parts of the body. These are the parts of the body for which the exercise was *not* intended.

Take leg lifts, for example. Leg lifts are when you lie flat on your back with your arms straight down to the sides. The legs are then raised to the vertical position, without bending the knees, and slowly lowered to the floor again. For the experienced student, leg lifts can be a piece of cake. They strengthen the muscles of both the abdomen and thighs. But leg lifts also put considerable pressure on the lower back. So, unless you are quite strong, supple and fit, you will actually be putting far more pressure on the lower back than on the abdomen and thighs! Build up to leg lifts by all means, through a balanced, regular exercise routine, but don't just rush straight into them, expecting to do ten in a row, if you've never done them before.

Aerobics can be Fun

The whole point of aerobic exercise is to do a sequence of movements, for about 12–30 minutes, at a steady and rhythmic pace, without stopping completely. The time you spend doing them depends on your state of fitness. But even the experts should not do them for longer periods than is sensible, otherwise they will get muscle fatigue. There's a limit to what our bodies can cope with even if we are in the peak of health and fitness!

If you are really puffed after a series of movements, then perhaps you shouldn't be doing them quite so ruthlessly. If you need a rest, then slow down but don't stop. Just do your jogging or whatever to a lesser, more shallow degree. But basically the speed and rhythm should be kept up and flow consistently. Playing some dance music often keeps people going.

Many aerobics classes have opened in gymnasiums and even local church halls, all around the country. Most of these involve doing a series of movements designed to stretch and work all parts of the body as well as supply oxygen to the heart and lungs. These include movements for making the joints supple and to stretch the arms, legs and torso.

Since the object of aerobics is to raise the normal pulse rate (the average for men is between 70–85 beats per minute and for women, 75–90) to well over 100 beats, they teach their students how to measure their own pulse rate and check it correctly.

Most of these classes have accompanying dance music. This is very useful as it gets the students all moving together and makes the whole thing a lot of fun (and exercise should always be enjoyable).

The following pages illustrate two kinds of aerobic exercise which can be done at home. They have been designed exclusively for the readers of this book.

Of course, you don't have to do them on your own. You could get two or three friends to join in and take turns calling out the movements.

The first set of exercises provide the basic "warm-up" routine. This is for the inexperienced beginner who needs to achieve some degree of stamina and suppleness before attempting the more advanced section. They should also be done by experienced students who need to warm-up their bodies before embarking on the tougher routines. The second, bigger section of aerobic work-out movements are for the supple, fit person.

Whichever set you decide to try, don't be put off by the fact that our model seems to be made of India rubber. She is a very experienced expert and now, after much practice, finds the stretches easy. What she is doing is demonstrating how the exercises can look in their ultimate, most perfect form. Most other people can't expect to achieve this standard until they have been practising a very long time. But, as I said before, you don't have to be made of India rubber to make exercise work for you.

These exercises are primarily for youthful, very healthy and supple people. They should not be attempted by those with heart or back trouble, or pregnant women. If you have any doubts as to their suitability, then turn to the easier exercises (which are by no means any less beneficial) in the California Stretch or Yoga sections. Consult your doctor for advice if you think it necessary.

If you are youthful and fit but have not tried this kind of work-out before, then do what you can without causing your body pain. Most of the movements can be modified to some degree, to suit different types of people. Start off with just a few selected movements for each part of the body and gradually build up into a more vigorous routine.

Stop Before You Drop.

Don't exercise when you are very tired. Although some exercises (especially yoga ones) can be very reviving and refreshing, the harder ones, which really work the body and muscles, will only make an over-tired body more exhausted and, under these circumstances, won't do a great deal of good in the long run.

It is interesting to note that most skiing injuries occur in the last two hours of a person's holiday. Keen skiers just can't resist one last run down the slopes before they leave for home; and this is when their bodies are most fatigued, their minds least alert to possible dangers.

The same thing can happen with exercise. It is tempting to push yourself when you are doing well but it could prove the time when you push yourself just that bit too far. Even the most experienced fitness experts are guilty of this and will testify to the minor injuries that can so easily occur. So stop before you drop.

Points to Remember

Don't work-out after you've eaten a heavy meal. It is best to do it on an empty stomach. If not, you could end up feeling very queasy indeed.

Do not exercise in tight jeans. They will restrict movement and make some exercises impossible to carry out. Instead, wear loose clothing such as a tracksuit or a stretchy leotard and tights.

Wear training shoes when jogging or doing other foot pounding work. These will cushion the soles of your feet and alleviate any jarring both on them and the spine.

Breathe rhythmically when doing the exercises, this helps your momentum.

If you don't want to stop and rest during your work-out but feel very puffed, then slow down but don't stop.

Remember, if you have a weak heart, back trouble, are pregnant or very overweight, then always consult your doctor before embarking on a routine of this kind.

Don't jump into a vigorous routine suddenly. Build up to it slowly and stop gradually.

When you have finished your routine, try some very easy, slow, relaxing exercises in order to let your body return to normal. A good set would be the Salute to the Sun postures in the Yoga Section. Do these slowly and gently, without exerting yourself. To finish, lie down on the floor, flat on your back and take some deep breaths until you feel quite relaxed and refreshed.

Take a hot bath before retiring. It relaxes the muscles and helps prevent aching limbs the next day.

Warming-Up

A

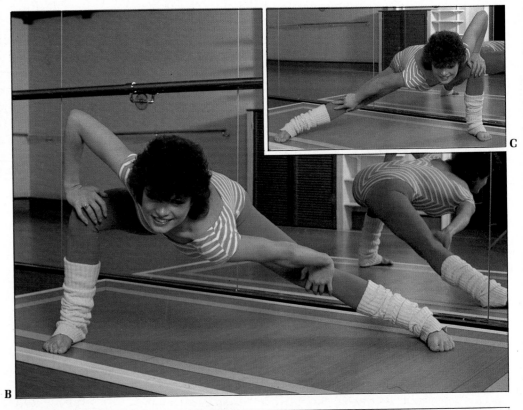

B

C

Exercise 1 ★

With feet wide apart and facing forwards, **(A)** knees bent, place your hands above your knees for support and bounce forwards and down ten times.

B and C

Make legs as wide as possible and, supporting yourself with your hands on your knees, lean from the waist to the inside of the thigh and bounce forwards and down eight times to the right, then eight to the left. Follow up with six to the right, six to the left, four and then two. Finally, do single bounces alternating either side ten times.

Exercise 2 ★

Now straighten arms in front (or bend them for comfort) and bounce into your bent groin the same number of times as exercise **1**.

Repeat on other side.

Exercise 3 ★★★

For advanced students – or the very supple! Put elbow on the floor and bounce for the same number of counts as exercise **1** and **2**.

A

B

C

Exercise 4 ★

A. Bend legs slightly and push your torso through, keeping elbows tight and returning to right-angle position between each bounce.

Now straighten legs (not illustrated) and push through eight times. **B.** Repeat with legs bent six times and legs straight six times. Then four and then two times.

C. Pushing through further.

Exercise 5 ★★

With feet firm and legs tense, push torso through legs and back ten times *without* returning torso to right-angle position with body.

Exercise 6 ★★★

With legs apart, take your chest over to your right knee, raise your left arm behind and pull to your knee for eight counts. Change sides and pull to left knee for eight counts. Now change to six counts either knee, then four and finally two. Finally, pull to each knee alternately for 16 counts.

Exercise 7 ★★★

Still in position as for exercise **6**, reach behind your right knee and, bending the arm that is on the floor, bounce down for the same counts as exercise **6**, finishing with 16 alternating, single bounces either side.

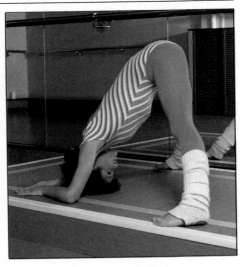

Exercise 8 ★★

Bend the left knee and, keeping the right knee tight, bend into the knee, twisting your body to hold the outside of the flexed left ankle with the right hand. The left hand is raised out behind. Now pull yourself towards the floor for ten counts. Repeat on the other side. Now alternate left and right for ten counts.

Exercise 9 ★★★

Bend the torso, straight at right-angles to the legs. Make sure feet are facing forward for support. Place palms down on floor, bend elbows and push down and up for ten counts. Advanced students may be able to touch the floor with their heads.

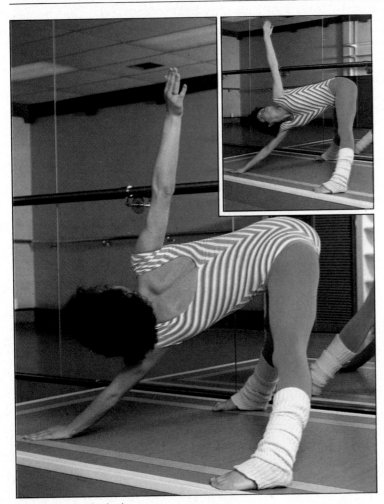

Exercise 10 ★★★

With arms straight, try to reach left then right ten times, taking the raised arm back in the opposite direction.

Exercise 11 ★

A. Crouching on toes with knees bent and arms straight in front, bounce eight times.

B. Widen legs as far as possible, try and place soles of the feet together. Keep arms straight in front and bounce eight times.

A   B   C

Exercise 12 ★★★

With one leg stretched out and toes pointing down to the floor, press down on elbows, gradually working them round to the outstretched leg **(B)**. Now push down on leg ten times **(C)**. Repeat with foot of outstretched leg flexed up.

Repeat both exercises on other side.

A   B

Exercise 13 ★★★

With palms flat on the floor – or as near as you can get, bounce twice in a crouched position then straighten legs **(B)** and take your head towards your knees **(C)**. Repeat both actions five times.

C

 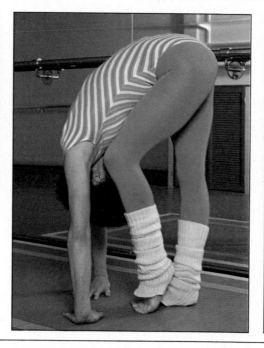

Exercise 14 ★★

With hands on the floor for support and head down, stretch each foot alternately keeping the other flat on the floor. Repeat ten times. Then straighten arms and legs and try to stretch both feet at the same time.

A

B

Exercise 16 ★

Start from a crouching position, knees bent, head tucked down to knees and very gradually unroll your body, keeping your chin down and raising your head last. Feel the roll in all parts of the body as you come up.

Exercise 15 ★★★

With legs straight, bend from the lower back and, holding your calves for support, try to pull your head and chest to your knees. Repeat ten times.

B. Now straighten your arms and grasp behind your knees, calves or ankles and stretch upwards ten times.

B

Exercise 18 ★

In the same position as **17**. Stretch to the left and straighten knees (**B**). Repeat eight times.

Repeat on right side.

A

Exercise 17 ★

With legs apart, bend knees and, keeping back straight, raise arms above the head. Interlock your fingers and turn palms out, towards the ceiling. Now straighten your legs and stretch tall. Repeat eight times.

A

B

C

Exercise 19. The Clock Stretch ★

Stand with legs wide apart, arms straight and stretch for the count of two. Now widen arms and count for two (**B**). Stretch arms to side for count of two and stretch arms at either side of hips for count of two (**C**).

Repeat going back up.

A

B

C

D

E

F

G

Exercise 20 ★★

Stand with legs apart, arms stretched out to sides. Bend knees and cross-over arms (**B**). Return to straight position (**A**). Repeat eight times. On the last count, reach up (**D**). Reach out to one leg (**E**) and hold floor either side for support, (**F**). Lightly bounce down to floor eight times then bend knee and lunge forwards (**G**). Gently bounce into this position eight times. Return to **F** and bounce six times, then **G**, six times. Repeat both exercises for four bounces each, then two. Return to position **A** and repeat whole sequence turning to other side.

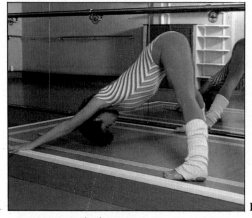

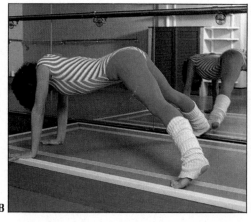

A   B   C

Exercise 21   ★★

With feet wide apart, arms as far in front as possible, pull back to heels eight times. Now move to position **B** and then **C**. Stay here resting on toes and hands and bounce hips to floor eight times. Return to **A** and repeat all exercises six times, then four and then two. Now do the whole movement in ten single movements.

Exercise 22   ★★★

This is an advanced exercise and few people should expect to do it as our model does. With legs wide apart, place one hand on the floor in front, arm bent with the other arm straight behind. Bounce torso towards the floor, bending from the waist. Repeat ten times.

Repeat on other side.

Exercise 23   ★★

Making body into a 'pyramid' position, bend one knee forward, pressing other heel down to the floor. Alternate ten times.

With both feet together, stand on toes then try to push heels down ten times.

Exercise 24   ★★★

Stand in a 'pyramid' position and kick right leg up behind ten times.

Repeat with the left leg.

A   B   C   D

Barre work

Exercise 1 ★★

Starting position. Stand with body in a straight line without curving back in. Clasp the barre with one hand, stretch the other arm out to the side.

B. Bending knees to the side, lower body keeping back straight.

C. Come back up and, straightening legs, raise outstretched arm over head in a side stretch **(D)**. Do this sequence 10 times.

Repeat other side.

Exercise 2 ★

Keeping one arm raised, stretch hips away from barre. Stretch over to wall again and hold for 10 counts.

Repeat other side.

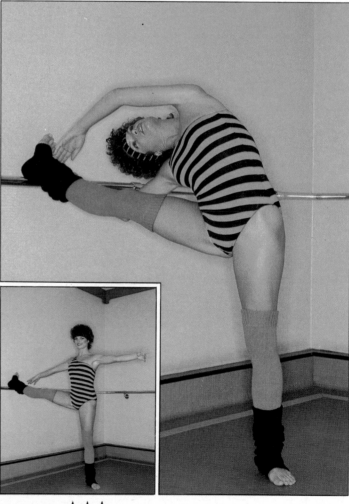

Exercise 3 ★★

Holding barre with other arm stretched out, stand with feet apart and bend knees. Now stretch over to the wall keeping torso to front. Hold for 10 counts.

Repeat other side.

Exercise 4 ★★★

Placing foot firmly on barre, try to keep torso to the front as you raise your arm and stretch over to the wall. Pull in to wall for 10 counts.

Repeat the other side.

Exercise 5 ★★★

Turn foot on barre forwards. Now bounce forwards for 10 counts (**B**). Now bend down and bounce through legs for 10 counts (**C**).

Exercise 5D ★★★

For advances students, bend right forward, place palms on floor and try to touch your knee to your forehead. Hold for the count of 10.

*Repeat exercises **5** on the other side.*

Exercise 6 ★★

With foot flat on wall above barre, bend into knee 10 times.

Repeat other side.

Exercise 7 ★

Facing wall, bend knee, place sole of foot on wall and bend back slightly.

Exercise 8 ★★

Keeping knee tight, leg straight, bend over to touch your forehead on your knee. Hold for 10 counts.
Repeat exercises 7 and 8 on other side.

Exercise 9 ★★

Facing wall with leg stretched out to side and right arm on barre in front, bend left arm up and over taking torso to outstretched leg (**B**).

A

B

Exercise 11 ★★

Standing sideways to barre, swing leg over to the wall and out to the side 10 times.

Repeat on other side.

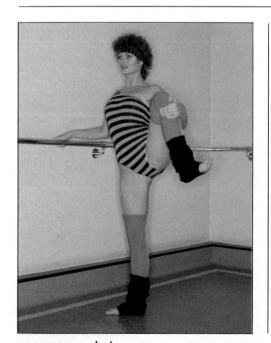

Exercise 10 ★★

Facing wall with right leg stretched out, slide right foot down the barre stretching the other leg behind. Hold for 10 counts.

Repeat the other side.

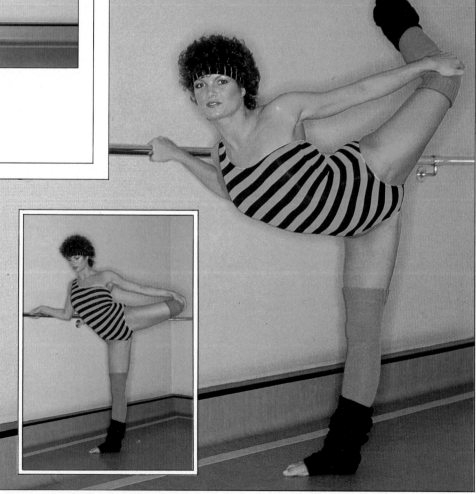

Exercise 12 ★★

Stretching knee up to the side of the chest, hold for 10 counts.

Exercise 13 ★★★

Only the very advanced student will be able to do this exercise holding their knee. The rest, grasp one ankle behind and, bending forward stretch the leg up and out behind. Hold for count of 10.

Repeat other side.

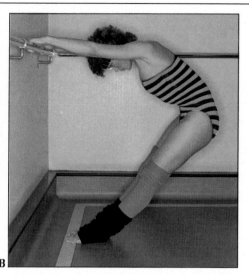

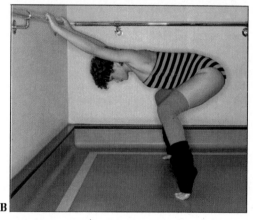

A

B

A

B

A

B

A

B

C

Exercise 14 ★

With arms stretched out on barre, stand about 18 inches away from the wall and relax down to crouching position. Hold for 10 counts.

B. Stretch legs with knees tight and, keeping head down, hold for 10 counts.

Exercise 15 ★

With legs apart and arms outstretched, face barre and bend to a right angle. Bend the knees slightly, thrusting buttocks up **(B)** and go onto toes. Rise and fall on toes for 10 counts.

Exercise 16 ★★

Stand two feet away from barre, facing wall. With arms outstretched bring knee up to forehead and kick up and back **(B)**. Repeat 10 times.

Repeat on other side.

Exercise 17 ★★

A, bend the leg that is on the floor and draw the raised knee towards the torso, then straighten. Repeat 10 times.

Facing wall, bend to right angle and bend outstretched knee. Lift knee up 10 times. **B** and **C.** With outstretched leg in position

Repeat on other side.

A   **B**   **C**   **D**

Exercise 18 ★★★

Stand three feet from the barre with back to the wall. Raise one leg and hook it into the barre behind. Reach down to rest palms on the floor.

B. Balancing carefully, reach up and back down again 10 times.

C. With one hand on the floor, twist your body and bring it round to outside of leg. Hold for 10 counts.

D. Bend knee and stretch further down to floor then straighten leg again. Hold for 10 counts.

Exercise 19 ★

Chest stretch. Standing three feet or more from the wall with hands together in front, balance on toes and, bending your elbows to the side, rest to the barre then push out 20 times.

Exercise 20 ★★

Standing with back to the wall, hands on barre behind, bend one knee and fall forwards. Bring feet together and hold out at angle from wall. Repeat eight times.

Repeat on other side.

Jogging

Exercise 2. The Achilles stretch ★

Jumping to each foot alternately stretch the
Achilles tendon for two counts.

Exercise 1 ★

Jump on the spot bending one knee behind and
touching each foot alternately for ten counts.

Exercise 3 ★

Kick legs alternately in front, 15 times.

Exercise 4 ★★

Kick leg behind, bending knee and kick it out
to the side. Do this ten times, alternating
the legs.

A

B

Exercise 5 ★★

Stretch out your arms and jump to the right, twisting your body to the left, then alternate for 20 counts.

B. Open legs and, jumping, twist from side to side for 20 counts. Then alternate exercises **A** and **B** ten times.

Exercise 6 ★

Keeping one foot flat on the floor, take the other onto the toes. Alternate 15 times.

A

Exercise 7 ★★

Jump feet apart, bend knees and stretch out arms, then (**B**), kick one leg behind touching it with the opposite hand. Alternate each foot ten times.

B

Exercise 8 ★★★

Clasp hands behind the neck and high kick each leg across your body to try and reach your elbow, ten times.

Exercise 9 ★★

Bend knees slightly, stretch palms in **upwards** clasp and twist waist by jumping **and pointing** knees from side to side, ten times.

Exercise 10 ★★★

High kick each leg in front clapping your hands
under your knee, 15 times.

Exercise 11 ★★

With your hands down to your sides, jump on
alternate feet trying to touch your bent knee on
your chest, 20 times.

Exercise 12 ★★★

Kick one leg out behind and, as it comes back
to the floor, kick the other leg out in front.
Repeat ten times.

Repeat on the other side.

Arms, bust, hips and waist

Arms, bust and shoulder area

Exercise 1   ★

To make wrists supple and strong, stand with arms straight out and flex up and down, 20 times.

Exercise 2   ★

Stand with arms out to sides and rotate wrists forward, turning arms, 20 times.

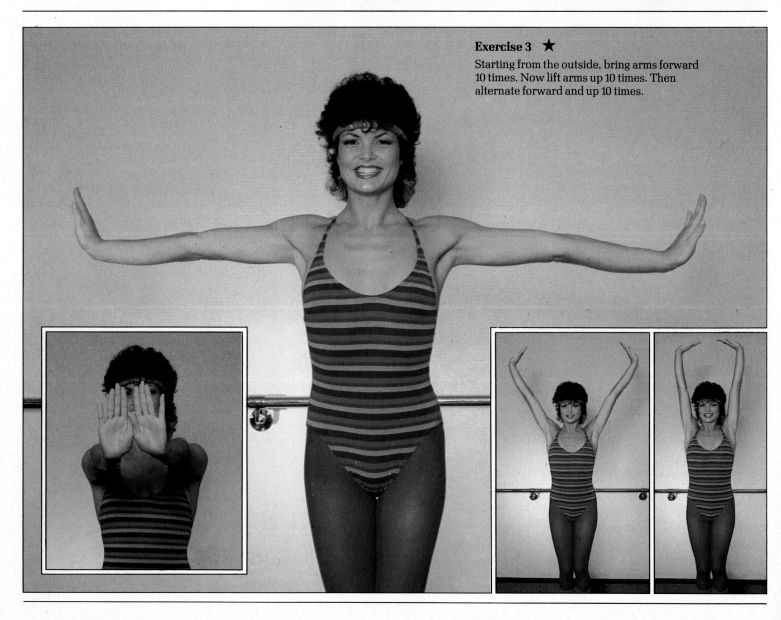

Exercise 3   ★

Starting from the outside, bring arms forward 10 times. Now lift arms up 10 times. Then alternate forward and up 10 times.

A · B · C

Exercise 4 ★

With arms at right-angles and hands crossed in front, swing them round to the sides (**B**) and then the back (**C**) trying to touch your shoulder blades together. Repeat 10 times.

Exercise 5 ★

Starting with hands down to sides, arms straight, criss-cross wrists over until arms are straight above the head. Cross up for six counts and down again for six.

Exercise 6 ★

Cross wrists over at front then swing round to cross at back 10 times.

Exercise 7 ★

Starting with arms out to sides, bend elbows and touch shoulders then back again, eight times.

Exercise 8 ★★

This is the same movement as exercise **7** but the torso is twisted to the left then the right at the same time. Repeat 10 times.

A

B

C

Exercise 9 ★

Knot hands into a fist, raise elbows and press palms together 10 times. Repeat to the left (**B**), now 10 times to the right and finally above the head (**C**).

A

B

Exercise 10 ★★★

Stand with feet wide apart and take torso down to a right-angle with the legs. Make hands into tight fists and, keeping elbows straight, swing out to the sides 20 times (**B**).

A

B

C

Exercise 11 ★★★

In the same standing position, make tight fists and pull into sides of chest, raising elbows (**B**). Now raise up and back (**C**) and take down to chest again (**B**). Repeat sequence 10 times.

Exercise 12 ★★★

This is a marvellous exercise for the back and shoulders as well as the arms and legs. Keeping feet firm and interlocking hands, take head down to the right knee with arms straight behind. Raise arms as high as possible. Repeat on left side (**B**).

Alternate sides 10 times.

A

B

A

B

Exercise 13 ★★★

Starting at the centre, drop from waist towards the floor and raise arms straight behind. Now rhythmically swing like a pendulum to the right knee (**B**), back to the centre and over to the left. Repeat sequence 10 times.

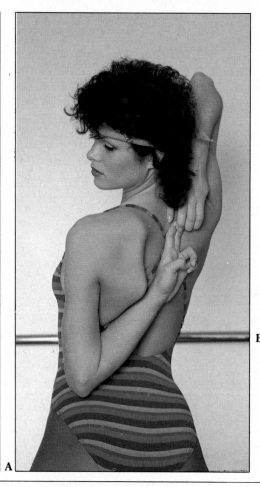

A

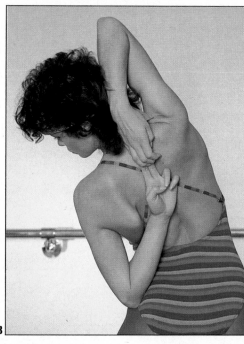

B

Exercise 14 ★★

For shoulders and arms. Standing with feet slightly apart, raise your right arm and take it over your shoulder to meet your left hand. (If they don't meet, then hold a piece of string or a handkerchief). Now pull over to the left (**B**), back to the centre and down to the right. Repeat 10 times.

For the Hips

Exercise 15 ★

For strength and mobility. Standing with knees slightly bent and arms down to the sides, flex the pelvis forward **(B)**, then back **(C)**, ten times. Don't move your shoulders as you do this.

Exercise 16 ★

Now thrust hips to the left side 20 times and then to the right 10 times. Keep shoulders still.

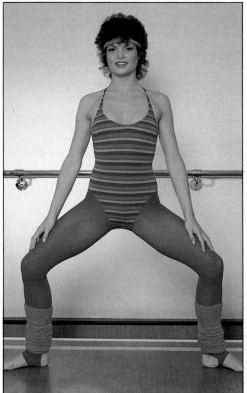

Exercise 17 ★

With legs wide apart, knees bent and back straight (not hollowed) thrust hips from side to side 20 times.

Exercise 18 ★★

With legs wide apart, knees bent, back straight, go up onto toes and raise arms above head, then thrust them to the sides and back to the first position again. Repeat 10 times.

A

B

C

D

Exercise 19 ★★★

With left knee bent, twist the waist and swing down to the left ankle placing the right wrist behind. Keep the left arm straight behind. Now swing down to the right (**B**). Repeat to the left again keeping the right wrist in front of the left ankle (**C**) and down to the right ankle again (**D**). Repeat sequence eight times.

A

B

Exercise 20 ★★★

Now repeat exercise 19 but with both legs straight. Repeat sequence eight times.

Exercise 21 ★★★

With knees tight and torso at right-angle to legs, twist your waist taking your right palm down to the floor, the left hand far behind. Look up. Repeat on the other side (**B**). Alternate, repeating 10 times.

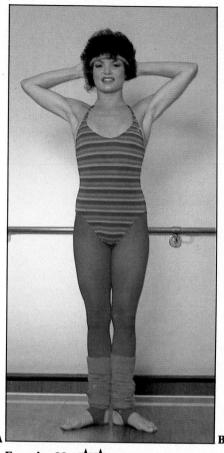

Exercise 22 ★★

Stand straight with hands clasped behind your head. Keep elbows out. Take your left knee up towards your left elbow **(B)**. Do not bend torso forward. Repeat 10 times.
Repeat on other side. Now alternate each side 10 times.

Exercise 23 ★★

Twisting your waist, take your right knee up to your left elbow. Repeat on other side. Alternate sides 10 times.

Exercise 24 ★★

With legs apart, toes pointing to sides, knees slightly bent, take your torso over to the left side **(B)**. Repeat 10 times. Now take it over to the right **(C)**. Repeat 10 times. Now alternate each side 10 times.

A   B   A   B

Exercise 25 ★★

Keeping elbows raised, fingers touching in
front, swing round to the left **(B)** eight times
and round to the right eight times. Repeat for
six counts, then four, then two. Finally,
alternate sides for 10 counts.

Exercise 26 ★★

Twist body round to the left, swinging arms
wide at the back as you go. Repeat eight times.
Now swing round to the right **(B),** eight
times. Repeat for six counts, then four, then
two. Finally, alternate sides for 10 counts.

A   B

Exercise 27 ★★

With legs apart, knees tight and keeping right
elbow bent back, reach down to the left 10
times. Now to the right **(B)** 10 times.

Exercise 28 ★★

Repeat exercise **27** alternating from side to side 10 times.

Exercise 29 ★★

Repeat exercise **28,** keeping one arm straight up as you reach down to the other side. Alternate 10 times.

Exercise 30 ★★★

Now repeat exercise keeping both arms straight above (obviously you won't be so mobile as our model).

For the Waist, Hips and Pelvic Area.

A

B

Exercise 31 ★★

Kneel on the floor with left thigh straight up and calf out behind. Straighten the right leg and, keeping torso to the front, take left arm up and over, sliding your right hand down to your ankle **(B).** Hold for 10 counts.

Repeat other side.

Exercise 32 ★★

In same position as exercise **31** but with right knee bent, clasp hands behind head and bend over to the right, trying to turn your chest up to the ceiling **(B).**

A

B

Exercise 33 ★★★

Sit on floor, legs wide apart, toes pointed, back straight. Stretch arms out to sides and reach over to the left taking the left hand down to the ankle (**B**) (Only the very supple will be able to put their left elbow *inside* the leg – the others rest it on the top). Hold for count of 10.

Repeat other side.

Exercise 34 ★★★

With legs wide apart, interlock the fingers and raise arms above the head, palms facing up. Now bend over to the right and hold for 10 counts (**B**).

Repeat other side.

Exercise 35 ★★★

Only very advanced students will be able to reach the floor.
Otherwise do not attempt to go that far. Just bend forward from the lower back as far as is comfortable and try to relax in this position.

Exercise 36 ★★★

Repeat exercise **34** with hands clasped behind the head and elbows wide apart.

Exercise 37 ★★★

Sit with legs wide apart, hands clasped behind the head. Twisting your waist to the left, bend your left knee and raise it to the right elbow **(B).** Repeat other side **(C).** Alternate 10 times.

A · B · C

Leg Stretching and Building Exercises.

Exercise 1 ★

Sit on the floor, toes pointed, palms turned out behind (or in if it's more comfortable). Now raise your body, taking your head back and jump legs apart and together again eight times. This exercise will also strengthen wrists.

Exercise 2 ★★

In the same position as exercise **1,** bend the left knee and kick up, across the body, six times.

Repeat other side.

Exercise 3 ★★★

In the same floor position as exercises **1** and **2** bend both knees and kick one up to the chest **(B)**, 10 times.

Repeat other side.

Exercise 4 ★★

Opening one leg to the side, lift it up and down eight times.
Repeat both these exercises on the other side.

Exercise 5

Sitting on the floor with legs straight, raise the right leg and, keeping the knee tight, draw it with your hands to your chest, then down again, for 10 counts.

Drawing your leg closer, tug it in, towards your face, for 10 counts.

B Keeping both legs straight in front, grip your instep and lift leg up and out to the side for 10 counts.

Repeat these exercises on the other side.

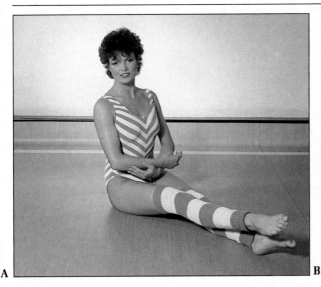

A   B

Exercise 6 ★★

Sit with legs straight in front and open one leg to the side **(B)** then close again. Repeat for eight counts.

Exercise 7 ★★★

A. Opening legs as wide as possible, turn your waist to the right, put your elbows either side of your knee and, bending from the lower back, pull your chest to your knee 10 times.

Repeat the other side.

B. If you can't get your elbow inside your knee, just rest it on the thigh, twist the waist back and take the other arm over the head. Pull down 10 times.

Repeat other side.

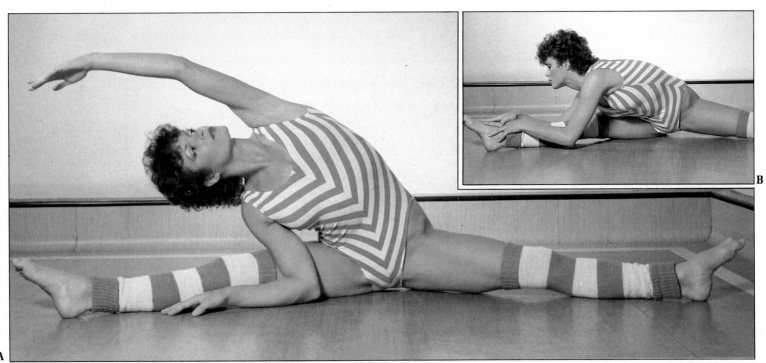

A   B

A   B

Exercise 8 ★★★

Sitting with one knee bent into the chest, straighten the other leg in front and flex the foot. Lift up and down for 10 counts.

Repeat other side.

B. Repeat exercise **A** but with toes pointed, for 10 counts.

For the Hips.

A   B

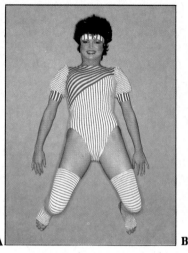

A   B

Exercise 1 ★

Lie on the floor with knees bent. Grasp ankles firmly.

B. Try and draw your right knee down towards the floor. Your body will automatically roll to one side.

Repeat with left knee. Draw knees down alternately 10 times.

Exercise 2 ★

Lie on back with arms to sides, palms facing down for support and knees bent.

B. Push hips up and move them to the right, trying to keep shoulders still.

Now move them to the left. Repeat alternately 10 times.

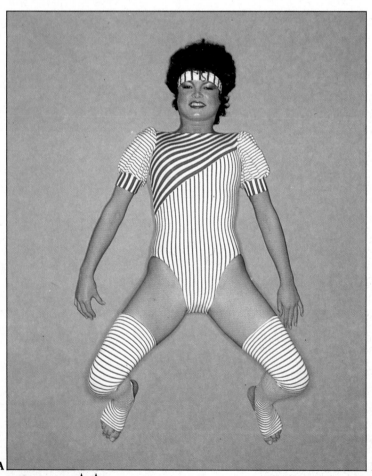
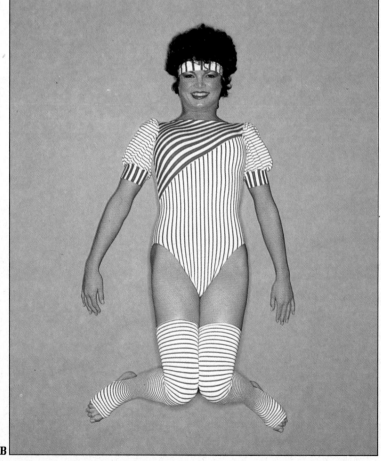

A   B

Exercise 3 ★★

Lie as for exercise **2,** knees apart. Arch hips up off the floor and open knees wide.

B. Now press knees together. Move knees in and out 20 times.

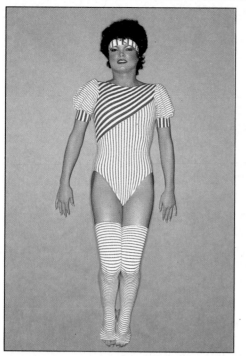

Exercise 4 ★★

Lie on floor, arms to sides, palms down. Place feet flat on floor and bend knees while lifting hips up. Rotating your bottom, move hips (*not* knees) from side to side 50 times.

Exercise 5 ★★

Lie on floor with feet flat and arms straight up. Knees are bent. Lift your hips (not your back) off the floor and tilt your pelvis up and back 50 times.

Exercise 6 ★★

With arms straight above and feet apart, take knees together and arch hips and back. Hold for 40 counts.

Exercise 7 ★★★

Lie on back with arms out to sides, palms face down. Bend knees at right-angles and lift gently up onto toes, then down again 50 times.

A

B

Exercise 8 ★★★

In position as for exercise **7,** go onto toes and kick up leg, keeping raised toe pointed, 10 times.

Exercise 9 ★★★

Now kick across body 20 times, with toe pointed.

B. Repeat exercise, 20 times, with toe flexed.

Exercise 10 ★★★

Supporting yourself on your shoulders and arms, go onto tip toe, raise one leg vertically and take it out and down to the side. Then raise back again. Keep supporting foot flat if neccessary. Repeat 10 times. ʻ

Repeat on other side.

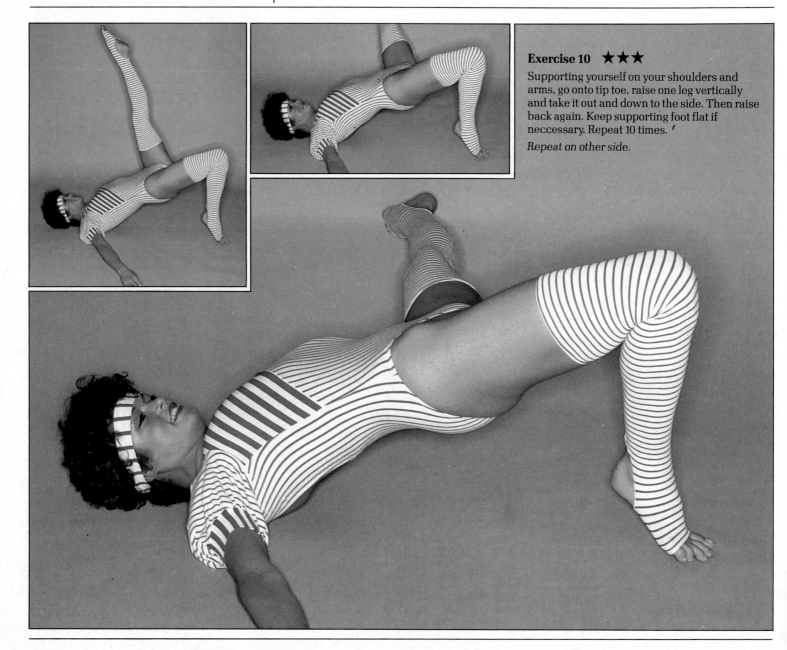

Exercise 11 ★★★

Lie flat on stomach, legs together, arms in front. Relax.

B. Keeping your head on the floor, take your arms behind you to grasp your ankles firmly.

C. Breathing in, pull hard on your ankles, raising your head and chest off the floor at the same time. Breathe out and try to relax into the exercise. Hold for 10 counts.

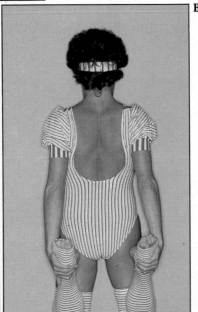

B

C

A

Exercise 12 ★★

Lie on your stomach, head raised, keeping elbow bent, the other straight for support. Lift left leg, point toe and take over to the right side. Repeat 20 times.

Repeat exercise with toe flexed. Now point and flex toe alternately, 20 times.

Repeat sequence on other side.

A

B

Exercise 13 ★★★

Kneel on floor with arms straight down, resting on palms of hands. Now raise left thigh up and kick leg towards the waist **(B)**. Repeat 20 times.

Repeat on other side.

Follow this last exercise up with a forward bend. Sit on the floor with legs straight in front and lower your arms to your ankles. Bend from the waist, trying to touch your forehead to your knees. Relax in this position.

For the Stomach

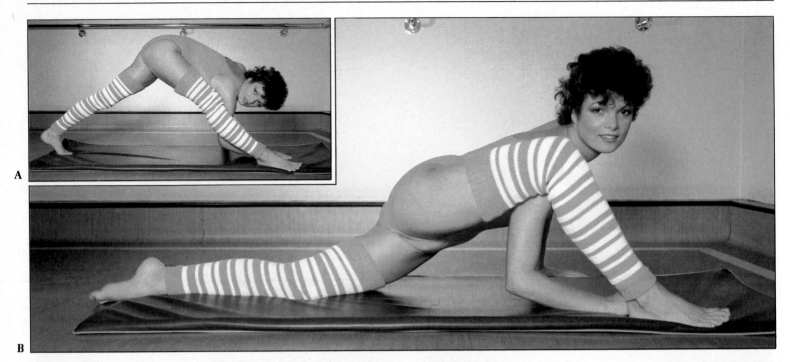

A

B

C

D

Exercise 1 ★★★

Stand with one foot in front of the other, legs wide apart. Take one elbow down to the floor. Hold.

B. Lower back leg so knee is on the floor. Hold.

C. Pushing back leg back along the floor, lower torso taking hand next to leg on the outside. Hold.

D. Taking arm on inside of front leg once more, stretch legs as wide as they will go. Hold. Repeat sequence on other side.

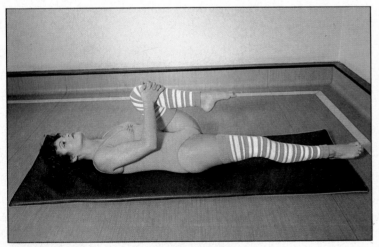

Exercise 2 ★

Lie flat on the floor. Tilt chin forward and drop head back to relax neck. Hug each knee up to chest five times then alternate six times.

Exercise 3 ★★

Alternately hugging each knee to chest, lift head and neck at the same time. Repeat 10 times.

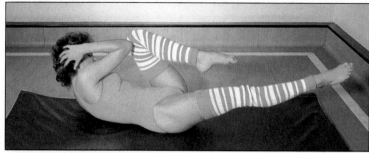

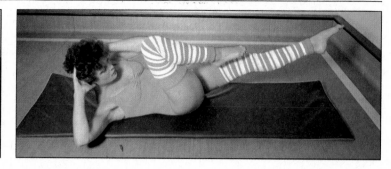

Exercise 4 ★★★

Clasp hands behind head, keep one leg stiff, the other knee bent to the chest. Lifting head and shoulders, touch right knee to left elbow and vice versa, alternating 15 times.

Exercise 5 ★★★

Lie flat on floor, arms stretched behind, one leg straight, the other knee bent with foot flat on floor.

B. Lift back, arms and straight leg, trying to put leg through arms to chest. Repeat eight times each side.

A

B

A

B

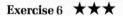

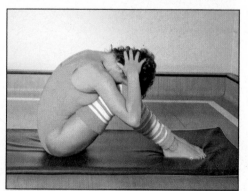

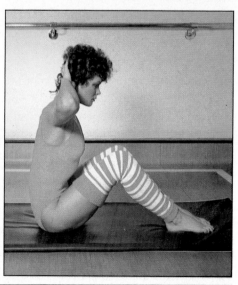

Exercise 6 ★★★

Lie flat on floor, legs stretched, toes pointed, arms straight behind head.

B. Lift back, arms and one leg, trying to put leg through arms to chest.

Exercise 7 ★★

Lie on floor with hands clasped behind the head and knees slightly bent. Now slowly sit up as far as you can go and back again, 10 times.

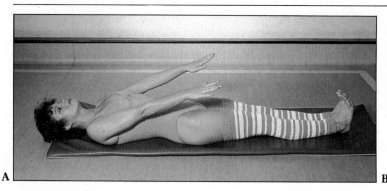

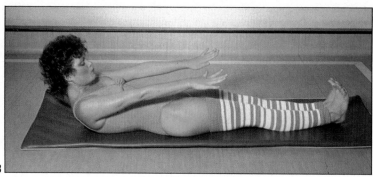

A   B

Exercise 8 ★

Lie on the floor with arms straight in front and
toes flexed.

B. Now pull forward 10 times.

Exercise 9 ★★

Pull head and shoulders up and reach hands,
alternating, to either side 10 times.

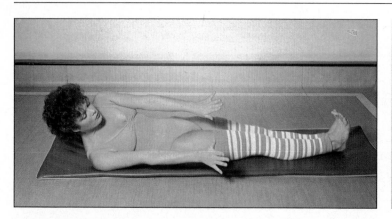

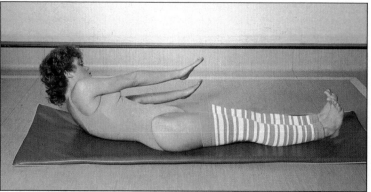

Exercise 10 ★

Hug knees into chest and relax.

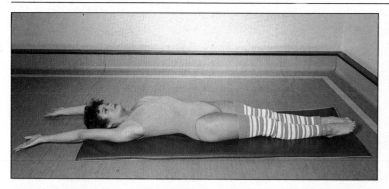

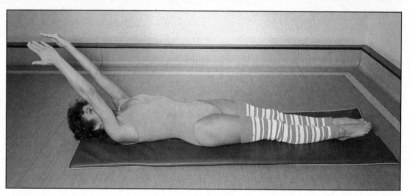

Exercise 11 ★★★

Lie on floor, toes pointed in front, arms stretched behind head. In one fluid movement, slowly raise back and arms to sitting position then go into forward bend. As you go back down, raise arms above the head again, then take them out to the sides and over to the back as you reach the floor.

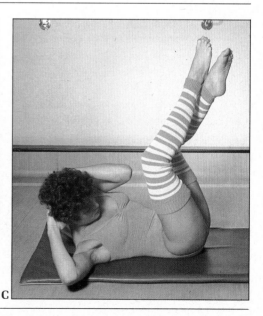

Exercise 12 ★★

Lie on floor, hands clasped behind head, legs vertical, knees slightly bent with ankles crossed.

B and C. Now raise head and shoulders and, twisting the waist, take right elbow over to left knee. Repeat on other side. Alternating, repeat 20 times.

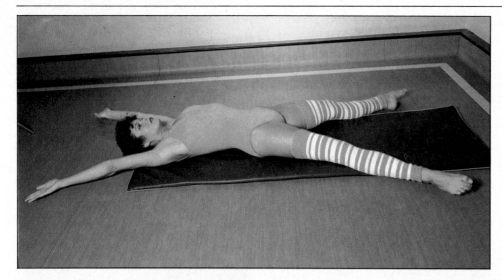

Exercise 13   ★★★

Lie on the floor, feet wide apart, hands apart behind head. Sit up and take head down to right knee with left hand on right ankle, right arm stretched behind. Now go over to opposite knee, taking left arm behind. Smoothly roll back to lying position.

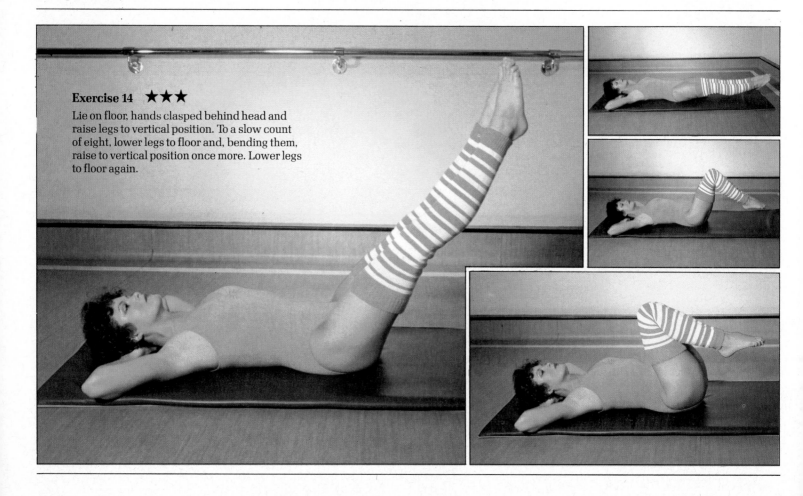

Exercise 14   ★★★

Lie on floor, hands clasped behind head and raise legs to vertical position. To a slow count of eight, lower legs to floor and, bending them, raise to vertical position once more. Lower legs to floor again.

Exercise 15 ★★★

Lie with arms down to sides, palms face down.
Raise legs to vertical position and cross ankles.

INSET. Twisting waist, raise head and
shoulders and take arm diagonally across to
ankles. Repeat on other side. Repeat,
alternating, 10 times.

A

B

Exercise 16 ★★

Take legs wide apart, raise them up and reach straight arms through, 10 times.

B. Keeping arms and legs stiff, reach over to the left ankle and then the right.
Repeat, alternating, 10 times.

Exercise 17 ★★

Lie flat on floor, legs stiff, arms straight behind.

B. Sweep up, raising one leg at same time and clap through to behind the knee.
Repeat, alternating, 10 times.

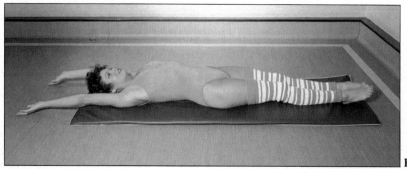

A

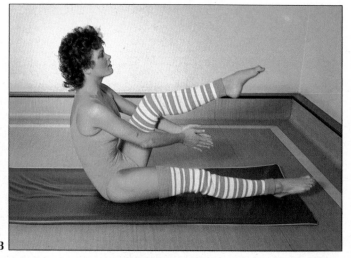

B

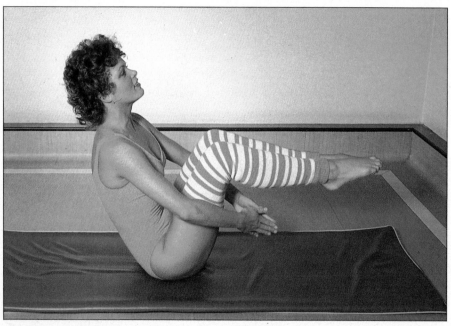

Exercise 18 ★★★

Lie flat and sweep back and both legs up to clap under knees. Repeat 10 times.

Exercise 19 ★★★

Lie spread-eagled on the floor and raise arms, back and legs at the same time. Try to touch ankles 10 times.

Leg Shaping.

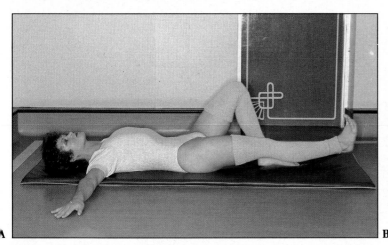
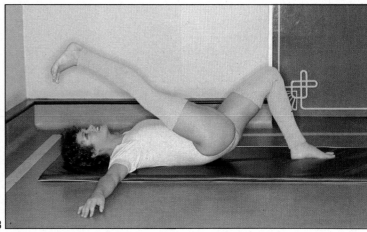

A   **B**

Exercise 1 ★

Lying on the floor with one knee bent, the other straight and arms stretched out to the sides, raise the straight leg up 10 times **(B)**. *Repeat other side.*

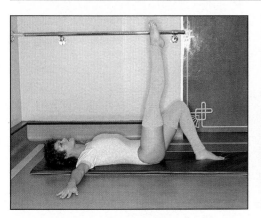
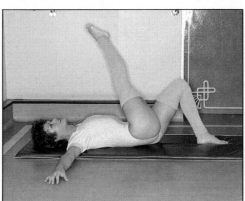

Exercise 2 ★

Point toes, take the straight leg over the bent knee and kick diagonally across for 20 counts. Repeat with other leg.

Repeat exercise with foot flexed.

Exercise 3 ★

Still with one knee bent, arms out to sides, take straight leg out and down to one side **(B)** then up again 10 times.

Repeat on other side.

A   **B**

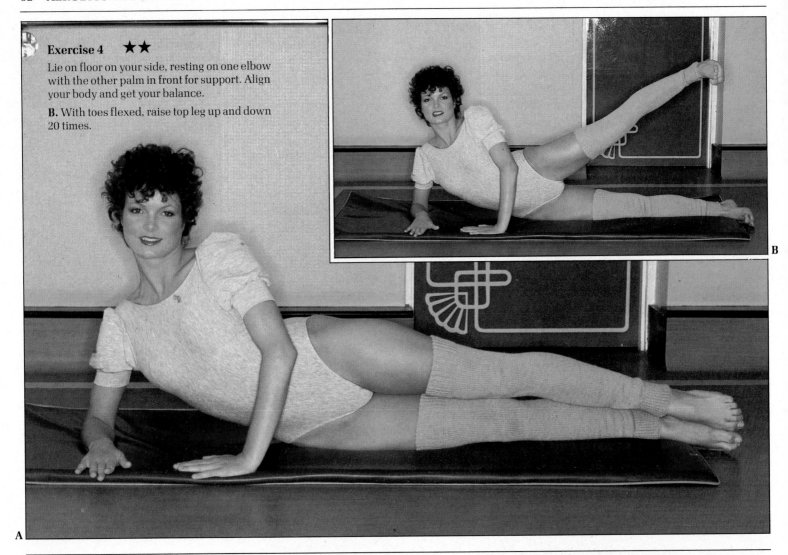

Exercise 4 ★★

Lie on floor on your side, resting on one elbow with the other palm in front for support. Align your body and get your balance.

B. With toes flexed, raise top leg up and down 20 times.

A

B

Exercise 5 ★★

Lying on stomach with one elbow bent, the other arm straight for support, point toes, raise one leg up and back then down again 20 times. Repeat exercise with toes flexed.

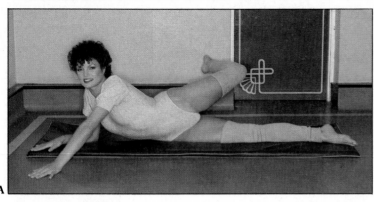 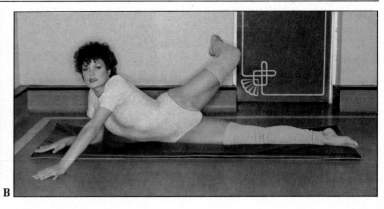

A
B

Exercise 6 ★★

In the same position, lift one leg up and back then down to the floor behind the other leg **(B)**. Repeat 10 times.

Repeat exercise on other side.

 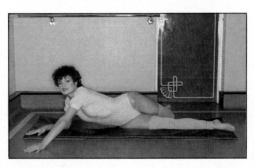 

Exercise 7 ★★

As in position for exercise **5,** bend one knee and lift leg up and back then down again 20 times.

Repeat exercise on other side.

Exercise 8 ★

Lie on side with both arms above the head, stretched out. Get balance. Raise top leg to touch top hand **(B)**. Repeat 10 times.

Repeat exercises on other side.

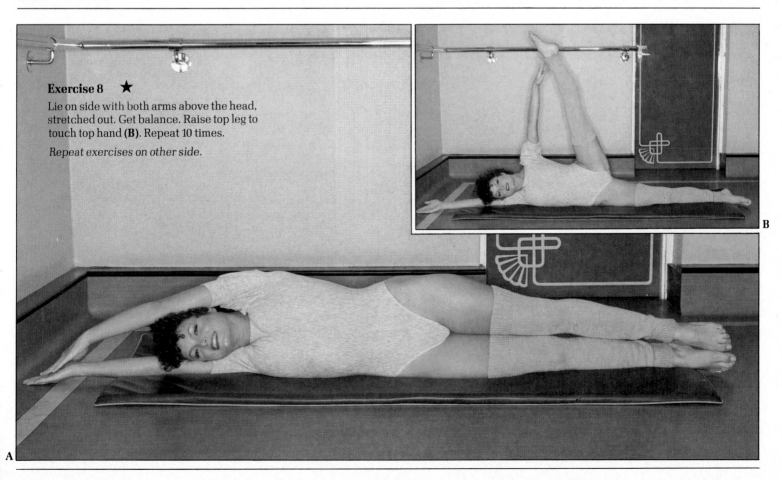

A
B

Exercise 9   ★★★

Lie on one elbow with other hand flat on floor for support. Bend one leg back. Raise other leg up and down again, flexing toes, 10 times. Lower straight leg to the floor and shallow bounce up and down 20 times.

B. Now push straight leg forward to waist level 20 times.

Repeat other side.

Exercise 10   ★★★

Kneel on floor with arms straight in front for support. Lift one leg up and out to the side. Point the toes.

B. Now try and kick leg up towards the shoulder keeping knee tight. Repeat 20 times without putting foot back on the floor. Now repeat with toes flexed up. Rest.

Exercise 11   ★★★

Now, with leg raised out to side, flex the knee and kick towards the shoulder **(B)** 10 times.

Repeat exercises 10 and 11 on other side.

Exercise 12   ★★

Still kneeling, arch back up and bring one knee towards the forehead. Now kick and lift it back and out straight **(B)**. Repeat 10 times.

C. Keeping leg out straight behind, toes pointed, raise it up 10 times. Repeat 10 times with toes flexed.

Repeat sequence other side.

Exercise 13   ★★

Still kneeling, go down to rest on forearms, hands straight in front and raise one leg up behind as far as it will go.

B. Bend the knee, pointing the toes over to the other leg. Repeat kicking movement 10 times.

Repeat on other side.

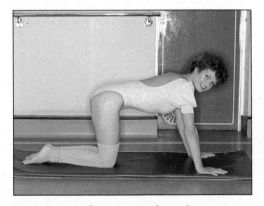

Exercise 14. The Catstretch.   ★

This limbers and relaxes the body after the leg work. Kneel on floor with arms straight, legs and arms are at right-angles to the body. Now, breathing in, arch back and neck, tucking head down, pulling abdomen in.

Relax breathing out, pulling tummy down, buttocks up and stretching head and neck back. Repeat six times.

The California Stretch

For those who love the idea of working-up a sweat through a heart-pounding aerobics routine but simply haven't got the stamina or suppleness to cope with a really vigorous work-out, then try the California Stretch.

This is a much more gentle, toned-down version of aerobics but, when performed with regularity, will still have just as much impact on your figure.

If you would like to increase your stamina, flexibility and eventually build-up to the tougher aerobic work-out pictured on the previous pages, try making the California Stretch programme a twice-weekly habit in order to prepare your body for the tougher exercises to come.

Warm-Up Head Roll ★

This exercise relaxes the neck area to prepare for the movements to come.
Sit in a cross-legged position and rest your chin on your chest. Now let your head drop back.

Slowly roll the head round to the right shoulder, do not strain. Continue circle to the left. Repeat on the left side.
Repeat 6-8 times.

The Exercises:

1. Aligning and Straightening the Spine ★

Lie flat, place feet together on floor and bend knees. Knees should be slightly apart. Place hands down to side, palms up.

Waist back: Tip pelvis back until the small of your back at the waistline touches the floor.

Ribs Up: Pull ribs towards your neck away from your hips without lifting spine from the floor.

Ears Up: Feel as though your neck is being pulled by your ears, away from your shoulders. Keep chin down at right-angle to neck.

Shoulders back and down: Keep shoulders flat on the floor and tug them down from fingertips towards your feet.

2. Basic Position for Abdominal and Pelvic Strengthening ★

Lying on floor, keep head and neck relaxed. Pin shoulders firm to floor, pull tummy in, keeping entire back flat on floor. Arms are relaxed to sides, palms up. Bend knees and keep ankles aligned with hips. Feet are flat, a few inches apart so ankles are in line with hips and knees. This basic posture alignment is maintained throughout the programme.

3. Full Body Stretch ★

To stretch muscles in waistline, upper hips, abdomen and back.
Lie on floor and extend arms over head, palms up. Legs are straight but relaxed. Stretch up with right arm and, at the same time, stretch down with right leg. Pull into a full stretch. Keep left side relaxed.

Now repeat on left hand side keeping right side relaxed.

4. Torso Stretch ★

To lengthen waistline and torso and stretch rib cage.
Lie flat on back with arms above head, palms up. Elbows are relaxed, knees bent, feet close to hips. Knees are slightly apart and spine firm to floor. Now stretch left hand up, hold and relax. Now right hand. Feel rib cage move.

5. Back Slider ★

To flatten upper back and firm bust.
Keeping thumbs on floor, slowly slide your arms up to shoulder level. Stop and check your waist is flat on floor, rib cage up, ears up.

Shoulders and back are down and relaxed. Now slide arms up above head, stopping every two inches, to hold, and press small of back into floor.

6. The Clinch ★

This strengthens pelvic girdle, leg muscles, firms tummy muscles, waist, thighs and buttocks.
Lie in basic, knees bent position, toes pointed down. Inhale and, with feet flexed, hug thighs to chest. Exhale, point toes and return to first position.

Repeat 5-10 times.

7. Pedal Stretch Upward ★★

To firm legs and pelvic muscles.
Inhale, pull right knee back to right shoulder, pointing toes. Exhale as you stretch left leg up to ceiling. Straighten leg and align it with hip socket. Flex ankles as though pressing pedals. Lower straight leg to the floor exhaling. Repeat 5-10 times, alternating legs.

8. Pedal Stretch Forward ★

Inhale as you pull your left knee to your left shoulder with toes pointing forward, this time. Exhale as you return to starting position.

Repeat right and left legs 5-10 times each. Shake legs and relax.

9. Gear Shift ★★

This improves flexibility of knee joints – but never strain your knees.
Assume basic position with palms facing up. Inhale, extending right leg straight up in the air

directly over hip joint. Point toes to ceiling. Exhale. Bend left knee, point toes and hug to hip. Alternate legs, inhaling and exhaling.

10. Spine Lift ★

To straighten and strengthen spine and straighten shoulders.
Assume basic posture and check waist, ribs,

ears and shoulders. Press down on hands and, keeping feet firm and apart, lift spine off floor – one vertabrae at a time. Eventually your body

is resting on your shoulders, head, neck, hands and feet. Press neck into floor. Slowly come down.

11. No Strain Pelvic Tilt   ★

Strengthens pelvic and abdominal muscles.
Keeping head, neck and shoulders relaxed,
slowly roll buttocks and lower spine up to
middle of the back. Slowly, to a count of ten,
roll back to starting position.

12. Boogie Legs Up   ★★

Extend arms out to sides at shoulder level,
palms down. Pull knees up to chest. Press
small of back into floor. Point toes and
straighten legs to ceiling keeping back on the
floor. Return to bent knee position and repeat
5 times.

13. Stretch 'n Flex   ★★

Strengthens pelvic and leg muscles. Makes
ankles, knees and hips mobile.
Inhale with arms out to sides. Exhale as you
bend knees to chest. Point toes to ceiling.
Inhale and exhale slowly as you lift legs with
feet flexed. Inhale and point toes again,
upwards. Exhale keeping toes pointed, bend
knees and return to starting position. With feet
on floor, flex toes up again.

14. Leg Lift   ★★

Strengthens muscles in legs, pelvis and
abdomen.
Assume basic position and check waist, ribs,
ears and shoulders. Hug left knee to chest.
Raise and straighten other leg then lower, 4-5
times. Keep spine on floor.

Repeat on other side.

15. Bent Leg Swinger ★★★

Assume basic position but raise your back, and rest comfortably on elbows. Bend then extend right leg up, pointing toes. Lower to floor again. Repeat 10-15 times.

Repeat other side.

Single Leg Swinger ★★

This is the same as **15** but you lie flat and keep working leg straight and toes pointed as you raise it. Repeat sequence with feet flexed.

16. Leg Circles ★★

To firm and shape thighs.
Lie flat and extend arms to sides, palms up. Bend left knee and raise right leg to ceiling. Circle right hip out and away from body going down to floor (but not touching it). Repeat 8-15 times. Repeat on other side.

Repeat sequence with legs circling in opposite direction.
Alternative: Raise back and rest on elbows. With one knee still bent, foot on floor, raise other leg and make small circles in the air 8-10 times.

Repeat other side.

17. Wide Frog Legs ★★
(Moves A, B, C and D)

Firms and shapes insides of thighs.
(If need be, support your back with a rolled towel.) Lie on floor and extend arms out to sides. Bend knees over chest and grasp inside of heels. Open legs wide and bend knees in – like a frog.

18. Frog Legs Two ★★
(Moves A, D, C and B)

For insides of thighs and knees.
This is the reverse of **17**. Assume pose for **17**. Now spread legs until they are bent like a frog and bend knees back to start.

C

D

19. V.I.P. or Inner and Outer Thighs ★★

Lie flat on back, arms out to sides for support, palms down. Raise legs to ceiling with heels together, feet flexed. Turn toes inwards and slowly spread legs wide, bring them back together with toes flexed.

20. Bike Pedaller ★★★

Lie flat on floor, arms out for support. Pull knees to chest and, with toes pointed, simulate bicycle pedalling. Repeat 15-50 times. Repeat with feet flexed.

21. Knee to Chest Leg Raise ★★

Clasp hands round left knee and hug to chest. Straighten right leg and lift to ceiling, slowly lower to floor but do not touch it. Repeat 4-12 times.

Repeat other side.

22. Mountain Climb ★

To tighten tummy.
Assume basic pose with feet flat on floor, knees bent. Place hands on thighs and inhale. Exhale as you slide hands up to knees while slowly raising your back. Hold and inhale as you return to the floor.

23. Tummy Tightener ★★

Assume basic position and check waist, ribs, ears and shoulders. Now slowly raise your back, sliding your hands forward on thighs. Hold. Inhale deeply and exhale. Hold, pulling stomach in and up under ribs.

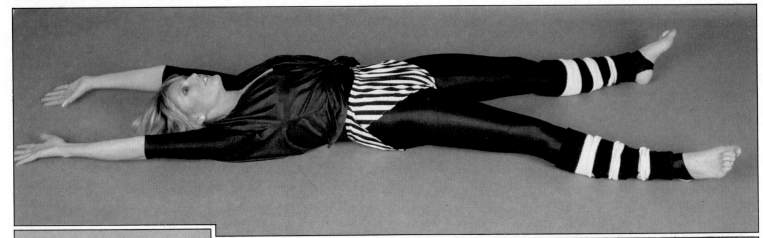

24. Upsy-Downsy Sit Up ★★★

To straighten and tighten abdomen.
Lie flat, legs straight, arms above head. In a smooth motion, swing arms up as you reach sitting position, bend forward taking right hand across to left foot. Relax as you lift left hand back. Bend knees as you bring hands together and roll back to floor.

Repeat other side.

25. Hip Roll ★★

For waist, upper thighs and abdomen.
Lie on back with arms out to sides, palms up. Bend knees to chest. Keeping knees together, roll them over to the right side so thigh touches the floor. Now pull knees towards elbow and hold. Return knees to chest and hold.

Repeat other side. Repeat 10-20 times.

26. Upper Hip Roll ★

To shape-up waist and upper hips.
Take bent knees directly over to opposite elbow and back to chest. Hold. Drop to other elbow and return to chest. Hold. Repeat 8-20 times.

27. Leg Cross-Over ★★

To shape waist and upper hips.
Lie flat on back, arms out to sides, palms up. Legs are straight and together. Raise left leg towards ceiling. Now cross it diagonally over the body and take to floor. Let hips roll and slightly bend both knees. Lift leg up again and return to starting position.

Repeat other side.

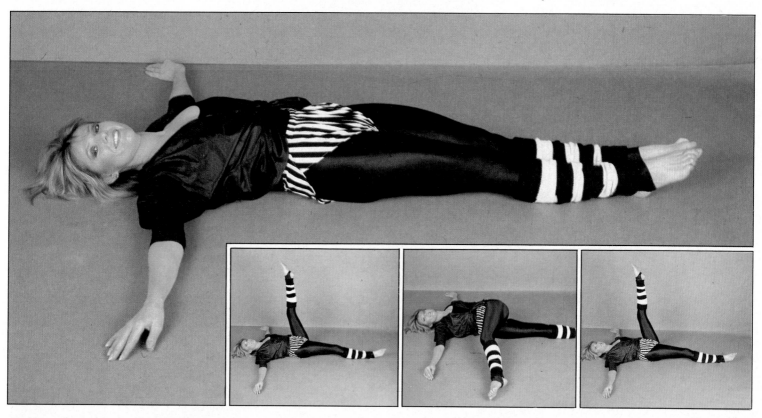

28. Bent Leg Cross-Over ★★

To shape waist, upper hips and insides of knees.
Assume starting position **27.** Bend left knee and lift to chest. Drop it diagonally over the body to the floor.

Repeat other side.

29. Tootsie Roll ★

Reduces lower hips, outsides of thighs and buttocks.
Sit on floor, back and legs straight, feet together. Place hands behind on floor. Roll onto left hip, resting on left hand, stretching right arm over head. Keep heels on floor, alternating sides. Repeat 8-20 times.

Tootsie Roll Plus ★★

Do the same exercise as before but with hands clasped above head and bending opposite knee. Repeat 8-10 times.

30. Hip Walk ★

To reduce buttocks.
Sit on floor, back straight, legs in front. Keeping arms raised, "walk" forward by lifting right hip and knee and sliding left foot forward then raising left hip and knee and sliding right foot forward. "Walk" forward 5-10 times and then "walk" back to starting position.

31. Side Stretch ★

To shape waistline, upper hips and loosen arm sockets.

Lie on side, arms over head. Rest head on arm underneath. Try to balance. With knee bent raise top arm and leg to touch. With knee straight, return arm and leg to floor. Repeat 8-15 times.

Repeat other side.

32. Side Biking / Side Scissors ★★

Reduces ankles, thighs, calves.

Side Biking: Lie on side, elbow bent, head resting in hand, place other palm in front for support. Raise both legs two inches off floor and pedal legs 8-10 times.

Repeat other side.

A

B

Side scissors: (Pictures: **A** and **B**) In same position, keeping legs straight and two inches off floor, "scissor" legs back and forth 8-10 times.

33. Upper Back and Elbow Reach ★★

For upper back and waist.
Lie flat on back, legs wide apart. Place fingers
on front of shoulders. Lift head off floor and
look at your toes. Roll across diagonally to
touch your left elbow to the floor (or near).
Keep legs and feet firm on the floor.

Repeat alternate sides 8-10 times.

34. Sitting Bends ★

For waist, upper hips, back and chest.
Sit on floor, legs wide apart. Raise arms and
clasp them above head. Bend right knee
slightly and reach forward from lower back,
taking arms toward right foot. Bring hands to
centre and take to left foot. Raise arms up
again. Repeat 5 times. Repeat taking arms
down to left foot, centre, right, then up.

35. Hand to Toe Bends ★

For waist and upper hips.
Sit on floor, legs wide apart. Bend forward from lower back until palms are on floor in front. Bend to left and clasp left foot, ankle or calf, with right hand. Take left arm behind. Reach to left and right 6-10 times.

36. Sit-Up Toe Reach ★★

For stomach, waist and arms.
Lie flat, waist pulled into floor, knees bent and slightly apart. Feet are flat on floor. Inhale and sit up reaching to ceiling. Exhale and reach for right toe. Return to floor. Repeat sequence to left toe. Alternate 8-20 times.

37. Sitting Waist Bends ★

For shaping waist line, upper arms and toning inner thighs.
Sit on floor, back straight, legs wide apart. Toes are relaxed. Take right arm out to side shoulder level. Left arm rest on left leg. Repeat 8-15 times.

Repeat on other side.

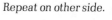

38. Standing Rope Climb ★

Two general, all-over loosening and limbering exercises.
Stand with legs apart, feet firm. Reach one arm high above head, then the other, alternating 12 times.

39. Side Bends Waist ★

Stand as in exercise **38,** bottom tucked in, hands on hips. Bend over to right and rotate torso round to back, left and front. Repeat 6-10 times. Repeat bending over to the left hand side first, then rotate.

40. Curved Arm Waist Stretch ★★

Stand with bottom tucked in, feet firmly apart, knees bent. Put left hand on hip, raise the right arm and curve it and the torso over to the left. Gently bounce down to the side.   *Repeat other side.*

41. Waist and Arm Reach ★★

Stand with feet shoulder width apart, arms gently curved in front. Drop head and shoulders to the right, reaching right arm to side and pulling left elbow up and shoulder back. Repeat on other side, then alternate, returning to first position in between. 8-16 times.

42. Waist Twister ★

For waist and midriff.
Stand with bottom tucked in, feet apart. Bend arms to chest level. Keeping hips still, twist your upper body twice to the left (doing 8 bounces), then twist to the right. Repeat 8-16 times.

43. Single Arm and Toe Touch ★★★

Good for waist and arms.
Stand with legs apart, knees slightly bent. Inhale and point right arm towards ceiling, left arm behind. Exhale and reach right hand to left toes. Left arm goes up behind. Repeat on other side. Alternate 8-16 times.

44. Toe-Touch Squat ★★

For waist, back, hips and thighs.
Stand with feet apart, bottom tucked in. Knees
are slightly bent. Stretch hands, palms
upwards, above head. Bending knees further,
touch hands to right foot. Stand up again and
touch hands to centre, up again and down to
left foot. Return to standing position and
repeat sequence 8-16 times.

45. Arm Swings ★

For toning the arms.
Stand with legs apart, knees bent, bottom
tucked in. Curve arms out to shoulder level
then curve back to cross over chest. Repeat
6-12 times.

46. Buttock Tucks ★

Stand with hands on hips, heels together, toes apart. Bend knees and tuck bottom in and under. Push hips and buttocks forward clenching muscles. Swing buttocks back and relax muscles. Now put toes and knees together and push hips and buttocks forward, clenching muscles. Repeat 8-16 times.

47. Buttock Tucks Two ★★

Pigeon-toed, swing buttocks back and relax muscles. Stand with legs together, feet straight, arms clasped above head. Tuck buttocks in and squeeze muscles tight. Now swing buttocks forward, tightening muscles. Swing back and relax the muscles. Straighten up with arms above head and hold. Repeat sequence 8-16 times.

48. Arm Series – 1 ★

To firm arms and loosen joints.
Stand tall, bottom tucked in, feet together. Take arms out to shoulder level and circle the arms forward eight times and back eight times. Flex hands up to ceiling, point fingers down and alternate 8-16 times. Relax arms. With arms out to shoulder level, bend elbows and take hands to shoulders. Flex hands, take down and circle to original position.

49. Arm Series – 2 ★

Stand straight, feet together, buttocks tucked in. Spread arms to shoulder level and flex hands to ceiling. Bring arms to stretch in front, and take above head. Repeat 8-16 times.

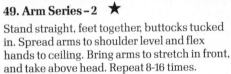

50. Arm Series – 3 ★★

Stand with legs apart, torso at right angles in front. Bend knees and make fists in front. Take fists up and out at back, as high as possible and straighten legs. Return fists to chest, bending knees. Repeat 8-16 times.

51. Bust and Arms ★

For firming and shaping the bust and arms.
Stand straight, feet apart. Grasp hands and raise elbows out to shoulder level. Pushing hands together swing to left, then round to the right. Repeat 8-16 times.

52. Shoulder Rolls – 2 ★

Stand straight, feet apart, Bring left arm and shoulder in front of chest. Repeat with right shoulder and arm. Repeat 8-16 times.

53. Shoulder Rolls – 1 ★

For relaxing the shoulders and loosening joints.
Stand with feet shoulder width apart. Hunch shoulders forward, arms straight in front. Swing arms back pushing bust out and slightly arching back. Hunch shoulders again, drop head down and stretch arms in front of thighs. Stretching neck back, swing arms back pushing chest out. Repeat, alternating, 8-12 times.

54. Chair Series ★

For feet and back.
Stand tall, bottom tucked in, legs together.

Hold onto chair for balance and go onto toes.
Lower right heel, raise and lower left heel.
Repeat 8-10 times.

55. Leg Work ★

For balance and to tone waist, hips and thighs.
Standing tall with right hand on hip, hold chair with left hand. Swing right leg from hip out to side. Hold. Swing leg out to front, point toe and return to first position. Repeat 8-10 times.

56. Leg and Upper Hip ★

To strengthen and tone joints and muscles.
With one hand on hip, the other on the chair, bring right knee up to chest and point toe. Swing bent knee back, hold, then return to original position. Repeat 8-10 times.

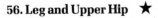

57. Back Work ★★

To strengthen and limber-up the back.

Stand with feet apart. Bend at right angles to chair and hold it for support. Bend knees deeply and sink chest in between. Tug downwards keeping back straight. Now straighten legs and pull downwards. Repeat 8-16 times.

58. Back and Inner Thighs ★★★

For mobility and increased muscle tone. Place left foot on chair so legs are at right-angles. Drop head and chest forward, with both hands on floor. Relax torso and pull towards right knee. Now reach for left ankle with left hand, keeping right hand on floor for support. Pull in to right knee. Pull in 8-16 times.

Repeat other side.

59. Waist Stretch ★★★

Place left foot on chair keeping right leg straight. Bend right arm over head to left knee. Pull down 8-16 times. Take both hands to left ankle and pull down to left knee 8-16 times.

Repeat other side.

60. Plié and Waist Stretch ★★★

With left hand on chair, keep heels together and turn toes out. Bring right arm up and over head. Now bring right arm out to side and bend knees. Repeat 8-12 times. Now, bending knees deeply, bounce down 4 times.

61. Buttock Kneel ★★★

For firming backs of thighs and buttocks.
Kneel on floor, resting on elbows. Without arching back, stretch out right leg from the hips. Point toe. Repeat with right leg. Repeat each movements 4-8 times.

Cool Down Series

62. Cool Down Squat ★

Squat down on toes with knees apart and palms flat on floor in between. Keep head up. Now bounce open and close the knees moving elbows in and out. Repeat 8 times.

63. Back Arch ★

To relax and unwind the back.
Relax onto knees, stretch arms at right-angles to thigh. Drop back down and arch head up. Now drop head and arch back up. Repeat 6-8 times.

64. All-Fours Pose ★

Resting on knees and hands, drop chest down. Spreading elbows apart, take head in between. Hold. Raise head back and hold. Repeat 6-8 times. Hold in final pose, inhaling and exhaling.

65. Roll-Ups ★

To relax the spine.
Sit on floor and, clasping arms round legs, rock back and forth. Repeat 6-8 times.

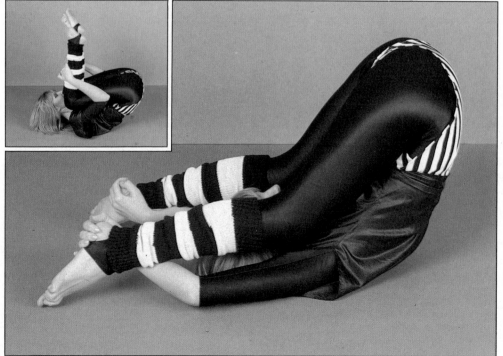

66. Spinal-Roll ★★

To limber-up spine and neck.
With hands inside insteps of feet, roll back and forth. Repeat with knees together, holding legs where comfortable. Repeat 6-8 times.

67. Plough Variation ★★

Lie down flat, arms to sides, palms down. Take legs straight up and push gently back towards head. Now take legs down to floor behind head. Bend both knees towards shoulders. Now bend and straighten both legs 4-8 times.

68. Variation on the Spider ★★★

Grasping insteps, widen knees either side of head and rock gently back and forth 4-8 times. Rock alternately opening and closing knees 4-8 times.

69. Forward Bend ★★★

For toning back and shaping-up legs.
Sit with legs straight in front, toes pointed. Inhale and bend forward from lower back, exhaling. Hold legs for support. Try to bring chest to knees. Hold.

70. Variation on Foward Bend ★★★

Sit on floor with legs straight out in front. Flex toes and hold them (or calves). Lift feet off floor and tug upwards. Now take legs wide apart and bend forward.

71. Spine and Leg Stretch ★★

Lie flat on floor, arms above head. Take both knees over to the left and then the right. Alternate 6-8 times.

72. Upward Stretch ★

Stand with knees bent, feet apart. Curve arms in front of chest then swing arms above head. Straighten legs. Repeat 6-8 times.

73. Forward Drop ★

Stand with legs together, arms above head. Pull up on toes and reach forward taking heels to floor. Drop torso and head down as far as is comfortable, bending from lower back.

74. The "Rag-Doll" ★

To relax and revitalise the whole system. Stand with feet apart (about 12 inches) and slowly drop forward bending the knees slightly. Stay in this position inhaling and exhaling three times. Now breathe normally.

Ballet Section

The professional ballerina has the kind of poise and grace many of us would love to possess. But this kind of movement takes years of hard training to achieve. Just because you didn't start ballet lessons when you were a child and will never hope to reach the kind of standard that's required for the stage doesn't mean to say you can't enjoy ballet by incorporating it into an exercise method.

Ballet exercises are one of the most disciplined kinds of physical movements there are. Every part of the body has to be positioned in a certain kind of way and the postures are held for a few seconds rather than repeated in breathless succession. The whole method will not only improve your suppleness but will also give you greater balance and a special kind of fluid grace.

Here is a programme of ballet-based movements that have been incorporated into an exercise method. If you find some of them hard to achieve, do what you can to start with and gradually build up your expertise.

A

B

C

Exercise 1 ★

First position: stand with heels together, feet turned out, legs and knees pulled upwards. Tummy is pulled in and back is straight. Arm is held in second position – slightly bent at elbow to curve forward at wrist.

B. Demi plié in first position: push knees out over feet as you bend them, keeping heels on the ground. Arm comes around to first position. Repeat eight times.

C. Recovering from demi plié, take arm out to second position. Knees are pulled up and held tight.

A **B** **C**

Exercise 2 ★★

Grande plié: Go through demi plié with heels together, feet turned out, knees angled over feet. Arm is in second position.

B. Grande plié with knees bent down so heels come off the floor. Arm comes down to curve in front. Keep knees from rolling inwards and turn them out over feet.

C. Return to first position through demi plié. Repeat four times.

A **B** **C**

Exercise 3 ★

Second position. Feet are turned out with knees tight. Arm is in second position.

B. Demi plié in second position: back is straight and knees are bent over feet. Arm comes down from second position to the front. Curve hand slightly inwards.

C. Demi plié, rising up to starting position, arm comes up to first position and opens out to second when straightening the legs. Repeat eight times.

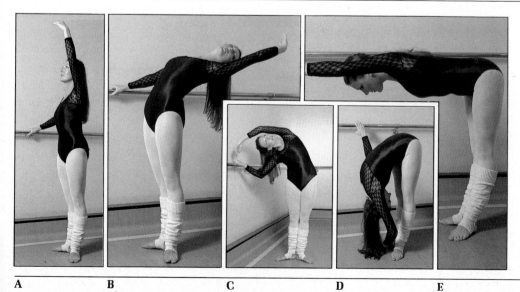

A **B** **C** **D** **E**

Exercise 4 ★★★

Feet are in first position. Arm is held in fifth, raised above the head with hand curving over.

B. Arch back and hold with arm above head.

C. Pull over to side towards wall with arm curved over head.

D. With legs straight, knees tight and feet pointing out, pull torso forward. Arm is still arched above the head. Tummy is pulled in. Repeat four times.

E. With knees tight, feet pointing out, bend forward in a straight line from the hips. Tummy is held in, back is straight. Remember not to sway backwards but to pull forwards over the legs. Arm is held out in fifth position. Now rise up to starting position **(A)** with arm still held in fifth.

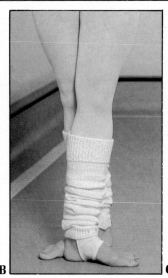

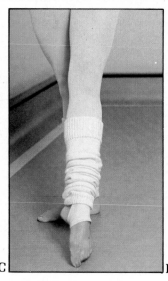

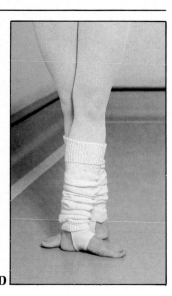

A

B

C

D

Exercise 5   ★

Feet are in third position (see **B**) with one heel against the inside of the other, toes turned out. Legs are pulled up and arm is in second position.

B. Feet in third position. Knees are tight and pulled up.

C. Tendu from third. One leg is turned out, the other toe is pointed with the heel raised and pushed forward.

D. Foot comes back and is turned out to third position again. Repeat sequence 10 times.

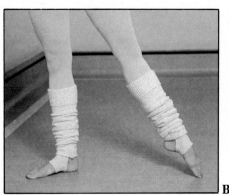

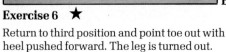

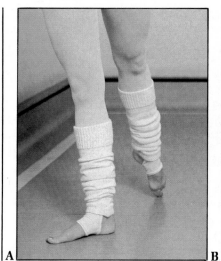

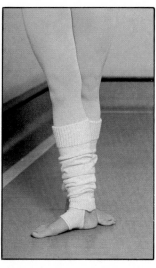

A

B

A

B

Exercise 6   ★

Return to third position and point toe out with heel pushed forward. The leg is turned out.

B. Close foot behind in third position and repeat 10 times.

Exercise 7   ★

Extend foot, pointing the toe and keeping the other leg and foot turned out. Keep the leg directly behind you and not extending out into second position.

B. Leg comes back to rest behind. Repeat 10 times.

A

B

Exercise 8   ★★

Return to third position with arm extended. Knees are tight and pulled up.

B. Leg extends to front with knee facing outwards, toes pointed. Tummy is held in and back is straight. Bring arm from second, back into third. Repeat eight times.

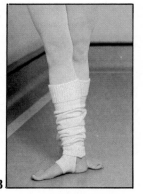

A B

Exercise 9 ★★

Leg is in third position with outside foot behind. Arm is in second.
B. Leg extends to 'arabesque' position.

Remember to hold torso over the standing leg and not sway to one side. Return leg to third position and repeat sequence eight times.

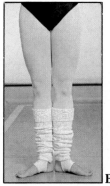

A B

Exercise 10 ★★★

Feet are in first position with heels together. Remember to keep knees tight and pulled up.

B. Bring foot up to passé position. Knee is turned out with heel of the raised leg pushing forward and toes pointed. Standing leg is taut with knee pulled up. Hold tummy in.

C. From passé position, bend knee near the wall, crook and raise other leg. Hand takes hold of heel of the bent leg.

D. Straighten body raising leg in front, then return leg to the first position. Repeat four times.

C D

A

B

C

D

Exercise 11 ★★★

Take leg out, hold under knee and point toe.
Keep standing leg turned out.

B. In same position, flex foot by pulling toes
upwards.

C. Bend both knees and take hold of foot
around instep, extend the leg still keeping both
bent. Make sure the knee of the standing leg is
still turned out over foot.

D. Still grasping the instep, straighten leg out
to the side. Repeat four times.

Exercise 12 ★★

Facing the barre, back and one leg is perfectly
straight while the other leg is extended over
the barre. Toes are pointed.

B. Slide foot out across the barre to widen
the legs. Return to starting position.

A   B

A

B

C

Exercise 13 ★★

Extend leg straight out behind to arabesque
position. Toes are pointed. Still keep both hips
facing the barre.

B. In the same arabesque position, flex the
foot by turning the toes to the side.

C. Keeping the leg raised behind, bend both
knees to 'attitude position.' Knee is lifted up

and out at the side. Flex toes to the side. Keep
hips facing the barre. Return leg to first
position. Repeat eight times.

A   B   C

Exercise 14 ★★

Supporting yourself with the back of a chair, stand in first position with hand on hip.

B. Extend leg up and out to the front. Keeping the hand on the hip enables you to keep the hip pulled back and down. Knee is turned out with foot pointed. Standing leg is again pulled up and turned out.

C. With knee bent, leg moves through first position to lifts into 'attitude position', and around to the back. Remember not to lift the hip up but keep pushing it down with the hand. Toe is pointed. Keep tummy pulled in. Repeat eight times.

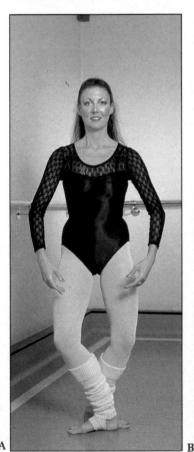

A   B

Exercise 15 ★★★

Knees are bent over feet, arms are held in second position.

B. Jump to straighten both legs in the air while arms stay in second. Return to original position. Repeat eight times.

Exercise 16 Jumps: ★★

Take up demi plié position with feet in third and arms curved in front.

B. Jump up keeping legs together, toes pointed. Arms are still curved in front. Return to floor with feet in third. Repeat eight times.

A   B   C

Exercise 17 ★★★

With standing knee bent and foot turned out, raise the other leg. Remember to keep the hip down and back.

B. Push up on toe straightening standing leg. Keep extended leg pushed out with the toe pointed. Arms are in second position.

C. Push up off the floor and onto toe. Return to demi plié position of supporting leg. Repeat eight times.

Exercise 18 ★

With standing leg turned out and pulled up, extend the other leg out to a right-angle. The hip is kept back and down with one hand. Point extended toe.

B. Swing leg back to arabesque position. Remember to keep leg directly behind you with toes pointed. Repeat eight times.

A   B

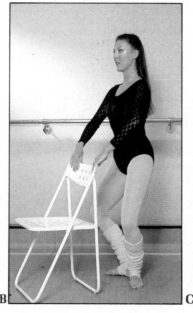

A   B   C   D

Exercise 19 ★

Standing behind chair with feet in first position.

B. Demi plié knees over feet remembering not to roll forwards.

C. Keep in demi plié position but push over toes to relieve stance, bending knees slightly.

D. From demi plié, straighten legs. Keep knees pulled up and tight. Tummy is in, back is straight. Return to first position bringing heels down to the ground. Remember to keep legs turned out. Repeat eight times.

A

B

C

D

E

F

Exercise 20 ★

Take up first position with arms curved in front.

B. Lift arms to right-angle in front.

C. Open arms out to second position.

D. Raise one arm up to curve over head.

E. Reverse arm position.

F. Lift both arms to curve above head and lower to the starting position again. Repeat four times.

Exercise 21 ★★

Keeping toes turned out, lunge forward opening legs. Knee should bend over foot. Arms are held in second position.

B. Lift arms to curve above head. Lean torso over front leg keeping bottom tucked in.

C. Now bend over front leg with arms still curved above the head. Repeat four times.

B

C

Working-out with Weights

One of the most exciting things to emerge from the current fitness cult is the fresh way women are being encouraged to regard their own beauty. Until now we have been conditioned to believe that good looks come out of an expensive jar of fancy face cream; that beauty can be bought over the counter in the cosmetics department of a large store.

There is nothing wrong with moisturisers, night creams and the like. They have their part to play in keeping our skin supple and preventing it from drying up too quickly. But they are certainly not the be all and end all when it comes to our looks.

We all know that the most valuable kind of beauty comes from inside. It roots itself in a feeling of well-being, happiness and lack of stress. It also comes from intelligent eating and from keeping the body and mind in vital, energetic working order through regular exercise.

These days it's fashionable to look happy, healthy and fit – and not just painted with expensive cosmetics. And looking fit does not mean looking *thin*. It means owning a firm, well-toned body that moves with suppleness and grace.

There's Grace in Strength

For many women, looking beautiful also means looking *strong*. This has nothing to do with bulging biceps and the kind of highly developed physiques that are found in weightlifting championships. But it does mean *developing* muscles and making them robust.

Building muscle – to a certain degree – makes sense. It can help counteract the flabby look so often present after weight loss. When you lose fat, the skin that has been stretched around it for so long tends to sag and hang in loose folds. This is because it has lost its elasticity through being expanded over fat. If, on losing weight, you gradually build-up the muscle beneath the skin, the result is a beautiful, firm, toned-up body that is no longer podgy but *is* curvy and well proportioned.

Building muscle does not mean ending-up looking like an experienced shot-putter. It does mean developing new shape in the body, achieving contour over buttocks, calves, thighs, shoulders and backs.

These days, many women are turning to the gymnasium to embark on weight training programmes. They are forsaking those electrically operated machines that endeavour to tackle spot reducing (often with a marked lack of effect) and are concentrating, instead, on using machines or weights that help build muscle in all parts of the body.

For a long time weight training has been the privileged domain of men. But now women are muscling-in on the weight training scene and are beginning to learn that they too can have beautifully developed, well-tuned bodies – without building huge physiques.

Weight training bears little relation to weight lifting. *Lifting* is when 'Incredible Hulk' type men strain to hoist huge dumbells above their heads. With *training*, much lighter loads are used. Some of the weights look very small indeed and are easily lifted in one hand. But when they are used in conjunction with exercise, they are extremely effective in firming limbs. These are lifted several times in succession, to really work the body, rather than hoisted just once.

If you decide to train, remember that muscle tissue is heavier than fat. So don't be dismayed if you gain a little weight after training for a while. Remember, inches are being redistributed and you'll soon end up in better shape than before. But if you *are* overweight, then you could combine the training programme with a sensible diet. Drastic 'crash' diets don't work well with training. You'll be using up a lot of energy and will need a vitality-producing quota of food each day.

The Stars Muscle-In

Many of the top female television and cinema stars are discovering the delights of building and re-shaping their bodies rather than just dieting to make themselves thin. Look at Jane Fonda, Raquel Welch, Joan Collins. All three would be the first to admit they are well past their first bloom of youth. Yet all three women have lovely, beautifully proportioned bodies that ripple with muscle beneath the skin.

Dallas star Victoria Principal is a firm fan of weight training. She is known to be proud of her muscles and has been quoted as lamenting the fact her arm muscles have been air-brushed out of her publicity photographs!

No wonder these stars of stage and screen are so enthusiastic. To be fit and strong is to be sexy, too. Apart from the fact that robust, supple bodies look so appealing, a well-worked-out body is likely to be a more physically sensitive one, too.

Women Body Builders

Many women are terrified of embarking on a programme of weight training because they think it will automatically develop their muscles to a huge degree. But this just can't happen. Men are capable of developing large muscles because they have a hormone called testosterone. Women, however, are actually less physically capable of producing muscle because their hormone oestrogen slows down development in this area. Training experts will reiterate the fact that it is extremely difficult for women to achieve highly developed muscles – however hard they try. And some women do try very hard to reach this goal.

Right now a whole new sports field is growing for women weight trainers who enter body building competitions. But these women work for years to win the kind of physiques they are aiming for. At the start of the competitive year, they decide which competitions they want to enter and build a whole programme of training and diet around these dates.

In order to expose their well-tuned muscles to their best advantage, they adopt careful, high-protein eating programmes that aim to reduce fat to a minimum and build muscle to maximum. Immediately prior to the competition they diet and body build to a highly disciplined degree. The kind of bulging, gleaming muscles seen on women body builders in magazines, only stay in that 'peak' for a few weeks. They are the result of fastidious dieting and training just before the competition. The rest of the time the muscles will, of course, be firm and developed – but not to such a pronounced degree.

But two work-outs with weights in a gym each week will never produce a competition-level body. So, if you want to firm-up your figure, go ahead and exercise with weights in the confidence you won't end up looking like Mr Universe!

Another point that is interesting to note about competitive weight training is the fact that many female contestants are in their late thirties and forties. It is usual for them to have children as well. Although they may be more muscular than the rest of us would want, their obvious physical attributes and their lack of excess flesh is a marvellous testimony to their sport.

As well as strengthening and re-moulding their physiques, women weight trainers insist the sport has many other excellent effects, too. They say it helps banish stress, improves the condition of their skin, hair and nails, makes their eyes sparkle and gives them a whole new, far more positive, outlook on life.

Re-shape Your Body

The most exciting thing about weight training is the fact it can actually *alter* your physique. This, of course, is where crash diets fail miserably. The traditional British pear-shaped woman who goes on a diet for a month finds she loses weight over her neck, bust and shoulders leaving large fatty deposits over hips and thighs. But weight-training – coupled, of course, with *sensible* eating will actually help to redistribute inches.

A prime example of physical change through training is Christopher Reeve, who starred in the film Superman. When Christopher won the part he stood six feet five inches and weighed only eleven stone – not a lot for a man of his height. By the time he started filming he weighed 15 stone and had a new-shaped body that was *firm* not *fat*.

With a carefully worked-out programme of special eating and specific training exercises, Christopher's shoulders were broadened and his torso and waist tapered.

The man who showed Christopher how to re-shape his body was training expert Dave Prowse, who has helped us with our weight training section illustrated on the following pages. Dave was British Heavyweight Lifting Champion for three years running and now operates a gymnasium in London.

The Dave Prowse Fitness Programme

On the following pages, fitness expert Dave Prowse takes you through one of his specially worked out routines. Before you attempt each exercise, make sure your feet are firmly positioned for good support. If you have any back trouble, take medical advice before attempting the exercises.

Exercise 1. ★

This warm-up exercise is for the muscles of the waist and lower back.
Stand erect, hands on hips, and move down to one side as low as possible, back to the upright position and then down to the other side as low as possible. Repeat the movement 50 times (25 times each side).

Exercise 2. ★

This warm-up movement series is for the lower back and hamstrings.

Start from an upright position with hands on hips. Bend forward as far as possible. Come up and arch backwards. Repeat 20 times.

Exercise 3. The Two-Hands Clean ★★★

This is the first of the weight-training exercises and is designed for the whole of the body as well as being an excellent fitness movement. A barbell is lifted from the floor to shoulder level in one movement and most of the work is done with the legs, arms and shoulders. If you get sufficient leg drive, you will automatically come up on your toes as in picture **8.** You will end up with the bar resting across your breastbone as in **9.** A great all-round exercise, it should be performed 10 times, then rest for 2-3 minutes, repeat a further 10 times, rest another 2-3 minutes, and repeat for a third and last set of 10 times before moving on to the **Dumbbell Press.** Working this way is known as the 'set and repetition' principle i.e. you have just finished three sets of 10 repetitions and this will apply throughout the exercise course unless otherwise stated.

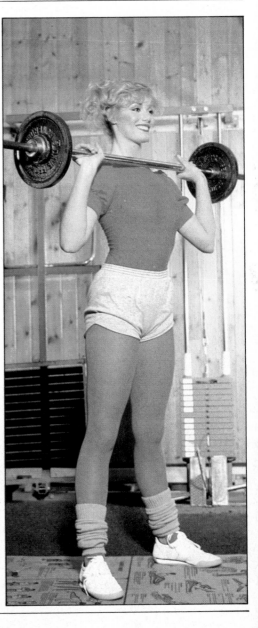

Exercise 4. The Dumbbell Press ★

Another arm and shoulder movement.
This is where the dumbbells are pushed from the shoulders overhead alternately. Do three sets of 10-15 repetitions.

Exercise 5. The Dumbbell Curl ★

Our next exercise is specifically for the fronts of the upper arms.
Stand erect, palms to the front, weights resting at the thigh and, by simply bending at the elbow, bring the dumbbells up until they touch your shoulders. Do three sets of 10-15 repetitions.

Exercise 6. The Grip Press-up ★★★

For the backs of the arms we use a table or, a low bench.
Lean up against the bench with hands fairly close together, thumbs touching. Keeping the body stiff, lower it until the bust or chest touches the bench, then return to the starting position. Most women are not very strong in this exercise, so do as many repetitions as you can, working up to 15 times.

Exercise 7. The Bench Press ★★★

On to the next exercise which is the first of the bust movements.
Lie on a comfortable bench. It will need to be about ten inches wide and somebody will have to hand you the barbell at arms length as performed in picture **17.** Take a hand spacing slightly wider than shoulder width and, taking a deep breath, lower the barbell down to the throat area, i.e. to the top of the bust or chest. Immediately start to push the barbell up to starting position, exhaling at the finish, and repeat the exercise 10 times. This is specifically for the big chest muscles and an improvement in your pectoralis region will result in an improved bust.

Exercise 8. The Flyer ★★

Our next exercise is also a bust exercise. This time we use dumbbells and we also utilise the bench again. Hold the dumbbells at arms length, lying on a bench. Take a deep breath and, keeping the arms fairly straight, let the dumbbells go downward and out to the side. Get as big a stretch across your chest muscles as possible. This should be done 15-20 times, making sure you inhale on the way down and exhale on the way up. Three sets once again.

Exercise 9. Bent Over Rowing ★★★

Our routine consists of two back exercises, the first of which is for the big back muscles. Stand with feet well astride and pick up the barbell with a wide hand spacing. Stand up straight. Now lean forward so the back is parallel to the floor and the weight should be about six inches off the floor. From this position and keeping the back as straight as possible, with no movement in the back area, pull the barbell up to touch your throat, lower it and then repeat 10 times. Once again, three sets will suffice.

Exercise 10. The Two Hands Dead Lift ★★★

From the lower back we do an exercise called the Two Hands Dead Lift which although with men has become a competition lift with weights up nearly 1,000 pounds being lifted, we are going to do with dumbbells. Basically all the exercise consists of is lifting two dumbbells off the floor, standing up straight and returning to starting position. This is for the lower back and provided you have nothing wrong in that area – e.g. disc problems – some heavy weights can be lifted. Three sets of 15 repetitions will suffice.

Exercise 11. Leg Raise ★★★

I am only including one tummy exercise in the routine. Not only does it affect the tummy muscles, but the hips as well. Lie on the floor or, better still, on a flat bench, and, keeping both legs fairly stiff, raise them so that your ankles are at a 90 degree angle upright. Our model, as you can see, goes well past the upright position and also you'll notice she's wearing weighted ankle straps to make the exercise more difficult. With all the exercises we do in the routine, if they start to become easy, you can increase the resistance or increase the repetitions. All the exercises we do in the routine must have sufficient resistance to make it difficult to perform the amount requested – three sets of 10 or three sets of 15. Increase the resistances only when the exercise becomes too easy. On the **Leg Raise** you should aim to do 100 raises in five lots of 20 in each training routine.

Exercise 12. The Squat ★★★

Finally we come to a marvellous fitness, thigh and hip exercise.

Once again you will see we have utilised dumbbells plus a small block to put your heels on. This is to help you maintain your balance. It consists of holding the dumbbells at the shoulders and doing deep knee bends. Squat as deeply as you can. Each exercise necessitates a big deep breath on the way down and an exhalation on the way up. At the end of 20 repetitions, you should be puffing and blowing quite well. Three lots of 20 will round off this brief weight training routine.

The Nautilus

The Nautilus system of using weights involves the use of highly sophisticated equipment. It is designed to eliminate the possibility of human error with weight training (e.g. positioning the body incorrectly) and many of the machines can be used for a variety of different exercises. Suitable for both men and women, each Nautilus machine is designed for a specific part of the body and the weights used can be adjusted to suit the individual's strength and needs.

The aim of this method is to make the individual fitter and stronger without increasing body mass. Although energy is used there will be no weight loss unless a specific diet is followed.

When embarking on the Nautilus programme you must make sure you are seated in just the right place, therefore the supervision of a trained instructor is desirable.

When using each machine, lift the resistance (the weight) for a count of two, pause, then lower it smoothly to the count of four. Try not to hold your breath while straining. Instead, breathe normally.

Each exercise should be performed for between 8 and 12 repetitions and you should start with a weight you can handle comfortably (but not too easily) 8 times.

A Nautilus work-out should take between 20-30 minutes and the time lapse between sessions should be 48 hours and not more than 96 hours. The following photographs were taken using the Nautilus equipment at the Hogarth Club in London's Chiswick.

A 'warm-up' on a cycling machine is a good way to prepare your body for the Nautilus programme.

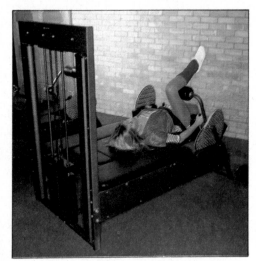

1. Hip and Back Machine.

Muscles used: buttocks, lower back, hamstrings.
Lie on back with both legs over roller pads. From bent legged position, extend both legs while pushing back with hands. Holding one leg fully extended, allow other leg to bend and come back as far as possible. Stretch. Push out until bent leg is extended with the other.

Repeat with other leg.

2. Leg Extension Machine.

Muscles used: fronts of thighs.
Place feet behind roller pads with knees against seat. Make sure head and shoulders are firm against back of seat. Straighten both legs to fully extend. Pause. Slowly bend knees to lower the resistance and repeat.

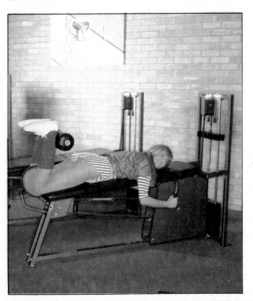

3. Leg Curl Machine.

Muscles used: hamstrings, buttocks, calves.
Lying face down on machine, place feet under roller pads with knees just over edge of bench. Grasping handles for support, curl legs and try to touch heels to buttocks. Lift buttocks to increase movement, pause then slowly lower resistance and repeat.

4. Hip Abduction – Abduction Machine.

Muscles used: outer hips and inner thighs.
Outer hips: With outer thighs and knees firmly against resistance pads, spread knees and thighs as wide as possible. Pause. Return to knees-together position and repeat.
Inner thighs: Place knees and ankles on the movement arms in a spread-legged position. The inner thighs and knees should now be against the resistance pads. Draw knees and thighs smoothly together. Pause. Return to spread-legged position and repeat.

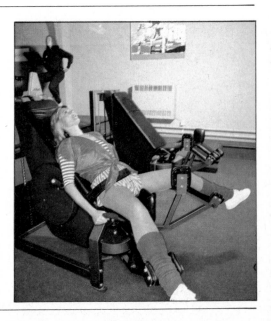

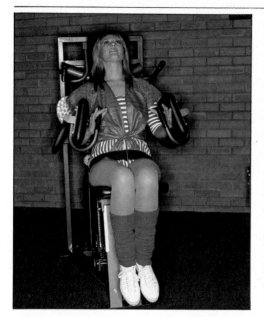

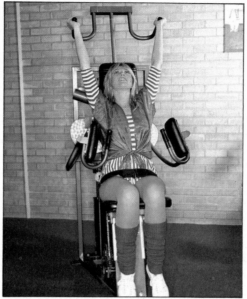

5. Double Shoulder Machine/Lateral Raise.

Muscles used: deltoid muscles of shoulders.
Pull handles back until knuckles rest against pads. Raise both arms from the elbows until parallel with the floor. Pause, then slowly lower the resistance and repeat.

6. Double Shoulder Machine/Overhead Press.

Muscles used: deltoids and triceps.
Grasp handles above shoulders and press them overhead. Slowly lower the resistance making sure to keep elbows wide.
Repeat.

7. Abdominal Machine.

Muscles used: abdominal.
Place ankles behind lower pads and sit erect. Grasp handles over shoulders and pull down, contracting abdominal muscles only. Pause in contracted position and return slowly to starting position.
Repeat.

9. Multi Curl Machine.

Muscles used: biceps of upper arms.
This machine can be used for a variety of arm movements e.g. **Two Arms Normal.** Place elbows on pads and curl both arms to the contracted position. Pause, then slowly lower arms to the stretched position.
Repeat.

10. Rotary Twist.

Muscles used: the oblique (side) muscles of the waist and the lower back.
The torso should be perfectly straight when attempting this movement. Sitting with ankles crossed for support and resting forearms on the pads, rotate the torso slowly to the right and come back with controlled movement.
Repeat on other side.

8. Double Chest Machine.

Muscles used: chest, deltoid muscles in shoulders.
Place forearms firmly against pads. Keeping head against seat back, grasp handles. Push forearms to try and touch elbows together in front of chest. Pause and slowly move arms out again with control.

Water work-out

Water–be it sea or swimming pool variety–must be one of the best places for a work-out. Because water is buoyant, it provides great support for the body. Exercises done in the pool become suddenly so much easier than when they are carried out in the gym or at home.

Swimming is one of the best all-round exercise methods there is. It strengthens the heart and lungs, improves muscle power, induces flexibility and generally gives you much more stamina. Water is also extremely relaxing. Even after swimming at a regular pace for half an hour or so, you will feel much more mentally soothed afterwards.

Swimming in the sea has the extra soothing benefits of exercising to the rhythmic sound and movement of waves. Sea water is also tremendously beneficial to the skin. Rashes and cuts often seem to clear up much more quickly when they've been exposed to the sea.

For most people, a seaside work-out is only possible once or twice a year–if that. The local swimming pool will prove the most accessible venue.

In some ways it's more practical to exercise in a pool. There is the bar at the side to hold on to when you are attempting exercises other than breast and back stroke. The trouble with most local pools is that they tend to get crowded–especially with small, energetic boys who never seem to notice other people when they dive into the water! Ask the attendants at your local baths when the quietest time of day is and try to make a point of going during those hours.

If you are not an experienced, strong swimmer, attempt widths instead of lengths, to start with. And take rests every so often. Try to get into a rhythmic way of breathing which will make the strokes easier and won't tire you so much. Vary the way you do the strokes when swimming a distance. For example, do six strokes in a slow, relaxed way, six more with strong bodily movement and then another six very quickly.

Any exercise method requires the right kind of clothes for comfort and ease of movement. And swimming is no exception. Visiting your local baths in the tiny strips of fabric you wore on the beach last year for highly inactive sunbathing could prove impractical. Instead, invest in a one-piece suit that offers plenty of support and opportunity for strenuous movement. And beware of the kind that looks very fashionable but ends up round you waist when you jump out of the water!

A

B

Exercise 1. For Legs and Abdomen. ★

Rest elbows on side of pool or grasp hand rail either side, for support. Keeping back and torso firm against the pool wall, straighten legs out in front and raise them to a right-angle to the body **(A)**. Now "scissor" legs wide apart **(B)** and then crossing over each other, alternately. Repeat 8-10 times.

Exercise 2. For the Waist.   (Right) ★

Turn side-on to pool wall and grasp edge with one hand. Feet are at the bottom of the wall. Keeping legs straight, raise free arm and reach up and over the head. Do not bend torso forwards or back. Repeat 8-16 times.

Exercise 3. For the Waist. ★★

Rest elbows on side of pool (or hand rail) facing
the wall. Straighten legs and keep them
together. Lift legs slowly to the right,
waist-level, and bring them slowly down
again. Repeat 4-6 times either side.

Exercise 4. For Legs and Abdomen. ★★

Stand with back to wall. Bend right knee and
lay foot flat againt wall. Stiffen left leg and
raise it up sideways, then slowly take it down
again. Repeat 8-16 times each side.

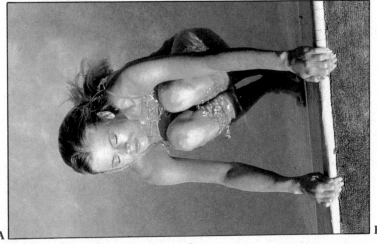

A

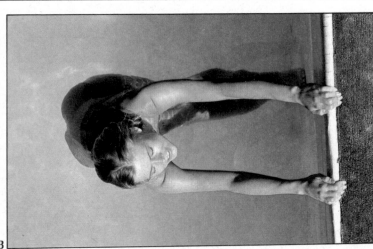

B

Exercise 5. For Legs and Arms. ★

Hold on to side of pool and, with knees bent,
place feet just below hands. Now stiffen knees
and straighten legs and arms (B). Bend and
straighten 8-10 times.

A

B

Exercise 6. For Legs. ★★

Stand at arms length from side of pool and grasp rail. Bend elbows and take feet apart placing them wide, either side of hands. Stiffen knees. Hold for 30-60 seconds (**B**) and release. Repeat twice more.

A

B

Exercise 7. For Abdomen and Thighs. ★

Rest elbows on pool edge (or straighten arms and grasp rail either side). Keeping back flat against wall, draw both knees up to the chest. Now straighten legs out, pointing toes (**A**). Open legs wide, flexing toes (**B**) and hold for a count of four. Now draw legs, in a circular movement, back up to the chest, bending knees. Repeat 8-16 times.

Exercise 8. Overall Stretch. ★

Stand against poolside facing wall. Bending left elbow, stretch left leg out far behind with knee stiff. Now swing leg to the right. Repeat on other side. Repeat 4-8 times each side.

Exercise 9. For Thighs and Upper Arms. ★★

Stand at arms length from side and place left hand on rail. Bend right knee, lifting the leg up behind. Grasp ankle or foot and gently tug right leg to your body. Repeat 2-4 times each side.

Beach Work-Out

Here are 26 holiday exercises for sun and sand. These can be performed early in the morning or late in the afternoon, when sun-bathing time isn't at a premium. Let the sand help you work-out and use your towel and beach ball as props too. They will enable you to return from holiday with not just a glowing, toasted skin – but a firm, well-toned body as well.

Exercise 1. For Thighs. ★

Sit up straight with hands behind for support. Dragging your heels against the sand, draw your knees up to your chest. (The sand provides extra resistance for thigh muscles). Now push legs out straight again and back in, 6-8 times.

B. Keeping in same position, drag one leg in while pushing the other straight out, against the sand. Repeat, alternating, 6-8 times.

Exercise 2. For Inner Thighs. ★

Still sitting with arms behind for support, push legs wide apart, digging sides of feet into the sand.

B. Now pull legs back to first position. Repeat 6-8 times.

Exercise 3. For Outer Hips and Thighs. ★★

Lie on your side supporting weight on elbow. Place one hand in front for support. Place legs at right-angle to body.

B. Move one leg up towards chest – using the sand as resistance. Move leg back down again. Repeat on each side 8-10 times.

Exercise 4. For Buttocks and Backs of Thighs. ★★

Lie down supporting yourself on your elbows, legs straight in front. Flex feet and dig heels into sand.

B. Now push legs apart, open and closed, 8-12 times.

Exercise 5. For Legs and Abdomen. ★★

Assume same position as for **4.**

B. Pull abdominal muscles in tight and burrow buttocks into sand. Alternating legs, drag each one up to the buttocks and back again, 8-10 times.

Exercise 6. For Waist, Arms and Bust. ★

Stand up straight with feet shoulder width apart. Straighten arms and drop ball above head (the ball will help you maintain your arm position).

B. Exhaling, stretch with control, over to one side and, inhaling, return to upright position. (Do not lean backwards or forwards.) Repeat 8 times to one side, then the other. Then alternate 16 times. (Knees may be slightly bent for comfort.)

Exercise 7. For Back, Backs of Legs and Buttocks. ★★

Bend knees and drop torso forward to right-angle with back perfectly straight (great for strengthening back muscles). Tuck abdomen in and straighten arms in front holding beach ball between hands.

B. Now straighten legs making knees tight. Repeat 4-8 times.

A

B

A

B

C

Exercise 8. For Bust and Upper Arms. ★

With feet shoulder width apart, bend elbows and clasp ball to chest level. Squeezing palms into ball, slowly move it round to the right (**B**).

Now move it round to the left (**C**). Repeat sequence 8-16 times.

A

B

A

B

Exercise 9. For Bust and Under Arms and Loosening Shoulder Joints. ★★

Standing with feet shoulder width apart, clasp ball behind head. Squeezing ball hard, move it round to the right (**B**). Now move it round to the left. Repeat 6-10 times.

Exercise 10. For Bust, Arms and Shoulders. ★★

In same stance as **9**, straighten arms and hold ball high above.

B. Now bend elbows and push ball down towards the waist.

A   B

Exercise 11. For Knees, Inner Thighs, Abdomen and Back. ★★

Lie on back, propped on your elbows. Squeeze ball tightly between knees and draw towards chest.

B. Pulling abdominal muscles in, reach up to clasp knees, curving your back. Hold for 4 counts. Repeat 6-12 times.

A   B

Exercise 12. For Upper Abdomen and Legs.

Lie on back, arms to sides, palms down. Bend knees to chest, holding ball between shins. Hold for 4-8 counts.

B. Now straighten legs and arms and reach up for the ball. Hold this position for 8 counts. Curve back down to sand then reach up for ball, 8-16 times.

★★★

Exercise 13. For Abdomen and Thighs. ★★★

(Do not attempt this if you have back trouble.) Lie flat on sand, arms to sides, palms facing down. Legs are straight up into the air with ball clasped between ankles.

B. Pressing down on palms for support, slowly roll legs down pulling abdomen in (do not arch back).

C. Bring legs down to sand and relax muscles. Repeat 8 times.

A   B

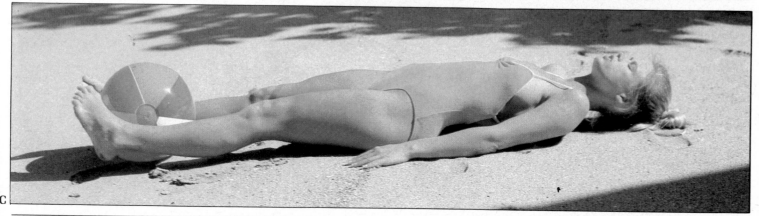

C

A   B

A   B

Exercise 14. For Hips, Thighs and Arm Strengthening. ★★★

Sit on sand with hands behind back for support (not too far back). Grip ball between knees.

B. Push up on feet and hands so calves and arms are at right-angles to torso and thighs. Do not arch back up. Squeeze ball tight and hold for 8 counts. Repeat 8-16 times.

Exercise 15. For Legs and Stomach. ★★

Lie flat on sand, propped up on elbows. Straighten legs and grasp ball between ankles. Now lift legs up to an angle with the torso. Hold.

B. Bend knees and take feet to sand. Straighten legs and repeat 8-16 times.

Exercise 16. Waist and Torso Toner. ★

Stand straight with feet shoulder width apart. Stretch arms above head grasping towel taut in each hand. Pull in tummy muscles and reach tall towards the sky feeling each joint and muscle stretch. Do not arch back.

Stand straight with buttocks tucked in and under. Grasp towel above head, arms straight. Inhale and exhale as you reach over to the left without bending forward or back. Keep hips central. Repeat 12 times each side.

Exercise 17. For Upper Arms and Shoulders. ★

Stand with buttocks tucked in and stretch towel behind your head.

B. Inhale, and bend right elbow, pulling towel over to the left. Alternately pulling and stretching to each side 12 times.

A   B

Exercise 18. For Shoulders, Legs and to Loosen Back. ★

Hold towel, one end in each hand, and stand on the middle of it. Keeping arms straight, look down as you pull up on either end of the towel. Hold.

B. Release tension in arms and bend down from the base of the spine. Return to first position and repeat 8 times.

Exercise 19. To Loosen Shoulders, Tighten Arm Muscles. ★

Kneel down on sand (but do not sit on heels, keep thighs straight up). Tuck tummy in and buttocks under. Thighs should be a few inches apart. Hold towel taut behind middle back. Stretch it out from both ends and hold.

Now, keeping the towel tight, bring either end to meet at front of chest. Repeat 12 times.

Exercise 20. For Shoulders Arms and Bust. ★

Still kneeling, hold towel in front of chest, one hand either end. Dig knees into sand for support.

B. Now pull towel hard, outwards. Repeat 12 times.

Exercise 21. To Loosen Shoulders, Trim Arms and Waist. ★★

Kneeling with thighs a few inches apart, knees dug into sand, grasp towel diagonally behind shoulders. Keeping towel taut, pull it up hard 16 times. *Repeat on other side 16 times.*

Exercise 22. To Tighten Legs and Make Back Flexible. ★★

Sit down with back straight, legs stretched in front. Flex feet and put towel round them holding each end. Pull the towel tightly towards the body. Point toes then flex and hold 8 times.

Exercise 23. For Legs, Abdomen and to Improve Balance. ★★★

Still sitting on sand with towel round feet, lift legs up keeping knees tight. At the same time tilt your body back until you can balance. Hold. Return legs to sand and repeat 8 times.

A

Exercise 24. For Legs, Stomach and Back. ★★

Sitting up with legs straight in front, step one foot into towel. Pull towel to body, stretching away with foot. Keep back straight. Repeat other side.

B. Assuming position as before, pull right leg up to chest, using the towel to lever. Keep back straight – do not curve it. Repeat 8 times each side.

Exercise 25. To Tighten Abdomen, Improve Balance, Make Knees Flexible. ★★

Bending arms and knees – but keeping back straight – tread into the towel and raise knees up to chest. Elbows should be out at the sides. Hold for 8 counts.

Exercise 26. To Tighten Abdomen and Make Legs Flexible. ★★★

Lie flat on sand and step feet into towel. Take legs up at right-angles to the body and tug towel to chest keeping knees tight. Hold for 8 counts.

Yoga

Yoga is the Sanskrit word for 'union' or 'oneness'. Originating in India, it is far more than just an exercise method. There are many different forms of yoga which involve development on a mental and spiritual level as well as bodily. Karma is the yoga of work and action, Mantra, the yoga of sound and vibrations through chanting, Bhakti yoga is the practice of devotion and love and Pranayama is yoga through breathing techniques.

The yoga method which is most popular and understandable in the Western world is Hatha yoga. This incorporates many hundreds of different postures for every part of the body, inside and out. Those who practice Hatha yoga say these carefully worked out postures (or asanas), which even include exercises for the eyes, tongue and scalp, will balance-up and harmonise the biological clockwork of the body, helping alleviate ailments such as backache and digestive disorders and clear the mind so it can function in a much more efficient way.

Yoga is recognised as one of the most powerful forms of exercise for combatting stress. This is why so many people who regularly practice it feel not only totally refreshed and revitalised after an hour's practice–but much more mentally rested and able to cope better with life's problems. Both aggressive types who tend to be over-active and those who are always tired and lethargic will find it equally beneficial.

Yoga is for All

The marvellous thing about yoga is that it is for everyone and not just the young, supple and fit. It suits children and can be practiced, to some degree, by the elderly or physically handicapped. Because of its soothing and therapeutic values, it is of tremendous use to the mentally disturbed and at least one London yoga society is campaigning to teach it in prisons.

We hear many stories in the West about the amazing feats accomplished by the Indian yogis. They are said to walk on hot coals, lie on beds of needles and even levitate. On a more down to earth note, it has been observed that certain yogis can reduce their breathing rate to one of two breaths each minute or raise it to 120 per minute. Others can lower their blood pressure and alter their heart rates at will.

These things are very hard for the Western mind to comprehend but there is no doubting the mental and physical discipline that can be achieved through lifelong, dedicated practice.

Many people think yoga is a passive exercise method that is very slow-paced and won't use up much energy. But this concept is misleading. Unlike aerobics, Hatha yoga is not an endurance method. Instead, the postures are held for a few seconds rather than repeated. And the more adept the student becomes, the longer he or she will hold them. But this often requires far more effort than just repeating an exercise several times over. It is quite usual for the yoga student to work up a sweat in class. The emphasis is on the *quality* of the postures undertaken and these can be very deeply penetrating indeed.

A Step to New Vitality

As well as massaging the internal organs of the body, yoga is very much based on stretching the muscles. As we grow older, unused muscles start to shrink and contract causing us to become stiff and bent. Yoga keeps the body beautifully lissom and supple, helps the back remain straight and posture erect. This is why so many yoga experts in their seventies look so lithe and vital.

One of the best things about yoga is that you don't have to be a double-jointed athlete to make it work positively for you. This is why it is so suitable for the old and infirm, too. All the postures, if they are practiced to *some* degree, however small, will work in a manner that is beneficial to your body. And don't think you have to be able to do a head stand or sit in the lotus position in order to make it effective. Some yoga positions are very simple to execute but extremely effective.

Since it is so powerful, the important thing about yoga is that you must be in the right position before performing any of the postures. For this reason, the best results will be achieved under the watchful eye of a trained teacher. Happily, the tremendously beneficial results of Hatha yoga are so widely recognised now, many local authorities run day and evening classes. The ILEA only recognise teachers who have completed an extensive course with The British Wheel of Yoga, so there can be no fear of being taught by someone who doesn't really know what they are doing.

Classes Vary

When embarking on Hatha yoga, remember that classes will vary enormously according to which teacher is taking them. Some teachers like to run rigorous classes while others prefer to go at a slow pace. Some teachers prefer not to teach headstands to beginners and others like to get their pupils up on their heads as soon as possible. At one class you might find the teacher chooses to devote half an hour to Pranayama or breathing techniques, leaving less time for the postures. Another teacher will concentrate on relaxation. The Iyengar method of yoga has been devised by B.K.S. Iyengar who runs his school in India. Although the postures are the same as any other yoga ones, they are tougher in that they are held for much longer. But most classes will follow a similar pattern. A short rest relaxing in the 'corpse' pose (lying on your back with your feet slightly apart and your palms turned towards the ceiling) is followed by standing postures, then sitting ones and finally those that are carried out lying down. At the end of the class there will be several minutes devoted to mastering relaxation techniques (very hard for the stressful beginner to adapt to at first!) All the postures will be carried out accompanied by a regulated breathing method for greater effectiveness.

Breathing is completely different in the yoga method. Most of us are accustomed to taking quite shallow breaths using the chest area only. With yoga, students are shown how to breathe using the abdomen. When they breathe in, they extend the abdomen so it rises into a curve. When they breathe out, the abdomen is slowly contracted towards the spine. Postures are carried out in combination with this breathing pattern.

Since there is such an emphasis on 'balancing-up' and harmonising the body, worthwhile teachers will encourage their pupils not to stretch very hard in one direction without doing a similar stretch in the other. This is why a series of forward bends is followed by backward ones or vice versa.

Another practice which is heavily stressed in Hatha yoga is balance. Many postures can only be perfected through good balance and it is astounding how many beginners to yoga find they can only stand on one leg with great difficulty! However, the effort is well worth it. Some students find mastering physical balance leads eventually to clarity and determination in thought as well.

With the emphasis on relaxation rather than strain, students are always encouraged to try hard but to relax into a posture at the same time. And the more they relax their joints and bodies, the easier the postures eventually become.

Because we are all built differently, not many of us can expect to carry out the postures in the same way. It is interesting to note, for example, that men often have difficulty with forward bends, whereas women, who tend to be more flexible in the hip and lower back area, can attempt forward bends more successfully. Few men, on the other hand, have trouble mastering a head stand and they often excel in postures which require strength in the wrists and arms. You will find there will be some yoga postures which come far more easily than others–depending on your frame, the length of your arms and legs, the flexibility of your spine. But don't just concentrate on the postures you find easy. Attempt the others as well–even if you can only hold them to a limited degree.

Before You Start

Here is a selection of yoga exercises for you to try at home. If you have a history of back trouble, either seek medical advice before attempting them, or work under the guidance of a qualified teacher. If you are a complete beginner, don't expect to be able to do them all correctly. Although you should naturally be putting effort into the postures, if you feel any pain while doing them, then stop straight away.

Remember, it takes years to become adept at yoga and even the most experienced enthusiast is likely to have difficulty with one movement or another. The photographs illustrate the kind of posture to aim for, but read the captions carefully in order to see exactly how you should be positioned. The very stiff, out of condition among you will not be able to do the forward bends very well–so just go as far as you can. And please don't be disheartened if that's not very far! Proficiency will come with practice. The very supple will probably find they can execute the postures better than our model!

The yoga exercises are divided into two parts. The first comprises a series of 12 movements which should be done in sequence. This sequence is called Salute to the Sun or Surya Namaskara, as it is known in Sanskrit. An effective, all-around routine, it is designed to stretch all parts of the body. It is traditionally done first thing in the morning (in the open air facing the sun–according to the climate!) and will revitalise and tone the entire body and mind, ready for the day's events.

Because this is a sequence of postures, the movements should flow naturally from one to another but each posture can be held for a couple of seconds or for a count of ten, depending on comfort. The idea is to start off with the feet in one place and end up with them in the same position.

You will see each backward bend is followed by a forward one. Try breathing in sequence to the movements. Breathe *in* extending the abdomen as you bend back and *out* when you go forward.

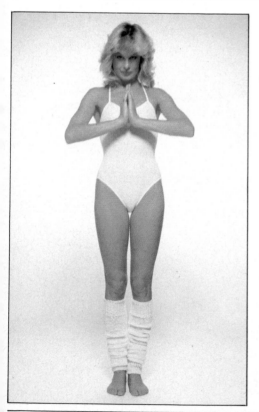

Salute to the Sun

Position 1. Stand with feet firm and together, toes spread forward and comfortably positioned. The back and neck should be in a straight line so check you aren't hollowing your back. Release all tension from the body. Place the palms of the hands together in front of your chest and inhale slowly and deeply. Hold breath for a couple of seconds and then slowly breathe out. This simple, positive stance prepares you for the work to come.

Position 2. *(Not Illustrated)* Keeping legs straight, breathe in and tip your body forward from the hips, stretching your arms straight out in front. Making a wide curve, take them back behind your head, stretching your torso back as they go.

Position 3. Keeping arms straight in front of you and knees stiff, breathe out while bending forward and reach towards the floor. If you have a stiff back and can only comfortably touch your knees, then don't strain further. If it is easy to touch the floor, bring nose and forehead to the knees.

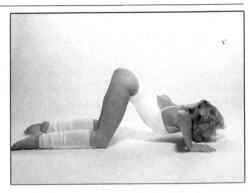

Position 4. In a single movement, bend your right knee and stretch left leg straight behind while placing your palms either side of your right foot. Arch your back and stretch your head back at the same time. Note the toes of the extended leg are inverted. Keep arms stiff. Feel the stretch in the front of the neck, the extended leg, the toes, feet and hands.

Position 5. Dropping the head to the front, move your bent leg back to meet the other one keeping arms, back and legs stiff and in a straight line. Press down hard on hands and toes for support. This strengthens arms and wrists and tones the leg muscles. For extra pull on the calf muscles, try to push heels towards the floor.

Position 6. With your hands and feet in the same position, bend your arms and knees and lower your chest to the floor with your head between your palms. Check your breathing is correct at this point. You should be breathing *in*! Now breathe out and then *in* again as you go into the next pose.

Position 7. Breathing in, straighten the legs and lift your head up and back. Your arms should automatically straighten and your pelvic area be resting on the floor.

Position 8. Breathing out, supporting yourself with your palms and with toes pointing in, drop the head to the floor and arch your back into the 'mountain' position. Keep the heels down on the floor and advanced students can try to touch the floor with their heads.

Position 9. Bending the left knee, bring the foot forward to rest squarely between your hands. Keeping arms and extended right leg straight, with toes inverted, arch the neck, head and back.

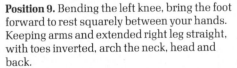

Position 10. In one sweeping movement, bring right leg to meet the left foot and straighten legs keeping the torso dropped forward.

Position 11. *(Not Illustrated)* Breathe in deeply, keep arms straight and sweep them forward, up and back in a curve. Stretch head and neck back at the same time.

Position 12. *(not illustrated)* Breathing out, return to the starting position and stand with palms together in front of your chest, legs straight and head, neck and back in a straight, tall but relaxed line.

Yoga Postures

Here are some more traditional yoga postures to try at home – and some postures that are based on yoga. Needless to say, you don't have to do the whole lot in one go! If you *are* trying several postures, though, take rests in between every three of four, in the 'corpse' pose. The object is not to exhaust yourself but to stretch, work and revitalise your body and mind. Always begin a yoga routine and end it with the 'corpse'.

Remember, never attempt too much – and if it hurts, STOP! Try to relax in a pose and *feel* the stretch. Attempt each pose only once unless otherwise directed. And don't rush. Just take each posture slowly, making sure you are in the right position first.

It would be ideal if you could get a friend to help you by reading the postures out while you try them.

The instructions are very important, especially since some of them are not suitable for people with back problems unless they are carried out under qualified supervision.

These postures are carefully planned. We have started off with some standing poses, then the floor ones on the back and finally those which are done on the stomach.

Remember, always treat your body with respect. Never attemp

the more advanced postures without limbering up first. It is a bad idea, for example, to go straight into the Shoulder Stand without preparing your body for this exaggerated movement. And this rule applies even to the most experienced student. So try to take the postures in sequence even if you don't do all of them.

Do not attempt these postures after a heavy meal, otherwise you will feel sick. It is best to do them three hours after a meal.

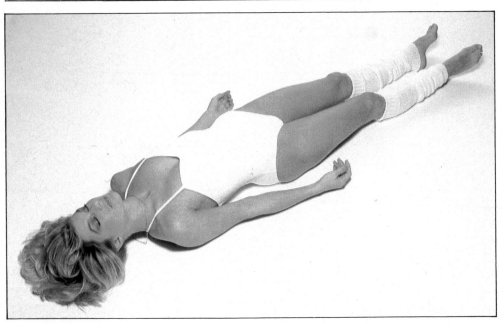

1. The Corpse Pose. ★

This is the basic relaxation pose of yoga. Lie flat on the floor, chin in line with pubic bone, feet a few inches apart and falling naturally outwards. Thighs do not touch. Arms are straight but relaxed and down, slightly away from the sides. Palms face upwards. (This has a more relaxing effect than when palms and fingers are touching the floor.) To relax the neck, shoulders and spine further, lift the head, tilt the chin slightly forward and drop the head back to the floor again. Breathe deeply a couple of times, then breathe normally.

You are now ready to commence yoga postures.

2. Variation of the Corpse Pose. ★

Lie in corpse pose, raise one arm above the head and move legs apart. Exhale, pulling abdomen and waist to the floor at the back. Inhale as you straighten and lift left leg, reaching for the left ankle with the right hand. Relax and repeat on other side. Good for stomachs and thighs. (Beginners can bend their raised knee.)

4. The Revolving Triangle. ★ ★

Stand with feet two and a half feet apart. Knees are stiff. Bend forward from the lower back and, turning your head to the right, try to grasp the right knee (if your are a beginner) or the right ankle (if you are advanced). Advanced students can also try to bring the chest or head to the right knee. Twist torso and look up at the ceiling. With one movement, sweep round to grasp the left ankle (**B**). Great stretch for the whole body: shoulders, neck, back, waist, arms and legs!

3. The Dancing Pose. ★

Stand in a straight position, feet firmly on the ground, toes spread. Raise arms above the head and place palms together. Keep elbows bent. Now gently move your head and shoulders over to the right. Press palms together and squeeze. Repeat on the left side.

This posture is excellent for poise and balance. The palm squeezing also helps improve the bust. To further improve your balance, stand on your toes before raising your arms and completing the pose.

A variation on this posture can be done to strengthen legs and back, too. With your arms above your head and your back straight, very slowly bend your knees and go into a squatting position. Squat as low as you can while keeping your back straight and stiff.

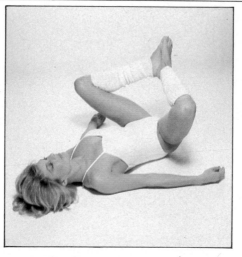

5. Tensing Posture. ★★

Start in the corpse pose. Now make balls of your fists and tense all muscles: calves, thighs, buttocks, arms and abdomen. Point toes, breathe in and exhale as you raise your legs, head, shoulders and arms. Keep arms and legs straight. Hold for a couple of seconds and release to corpse pose again. Relax totally. This posture tones all the muscles and then, through the releasing action, relaxes the entire body.

6. Knee Bend in Corpse Pose. ★

Lie in corpse pose and either ball hands or press palms down on floor for support. Exhale while pulling back and waist into floor. Bend your knees, join the soles of your feet and inhale as you pull your knees apart and towards the chest. This is excellent for limbering-up the pelvic area and lower spine while stretching insides of thighs. Exhale and release.

7. Leg Flex in Corpse Pose. ★

This is not suitable for people with back problems since it puts pressure on the lower spine.
Stretch arms out to sides so they are in line with shoulders. Place palms down on the floor for support. Pull waist and back into the floor. Bend knees to join soles of the feet and, keeping them stretched out as much as possible, inhale as you try to lift your legs. Exhale as you release and return them to the floor. Repeat a few times.

8. The Spinal Twist. ★★

Sit with both legs straight out in front. Bend the left knee then, keeping the knee on the floor, draw the left foot round under the right buttock. Now bend the right knee and step over the left knee so foot rests on the other side of the left knee. Straighten the back and check you have all the directions correct so far. It is very easy to do this posture the wrong way. With your back straight, twist the trunk, neck and head round to the right, so the abdomen is pressed against the thigh. Put your right palm on the floor behind you so it is in line with your hips and legs. Bring your left elbow over your right knee and clasp your left ankle. Breathe in and out deeply three times. As well as massaging the abdominal muscles and intestines, this stretches the thighs, neck, waist and back. It also loosens the shoulder joints.

Remember to repeat the posture on the other side.

9. The Cat Stretch. ★

Kneel on the floor, arms straight, palms down, with arms and thighs at right angles to the body. Inhale deeply, stretch head up and back and arch the body. Exhale, drop head down and arch the back up into a hump. Repeat several times. Very relaxing for the back, neck and spine. A good limbering-up pose.

10. The Tiger. ★★

Take up position as at start of **9.** Drop head and bring left knee up to the chin. Inhale and stretch head back while taking leg up and out behind. Keep knee tight. Exhale, drop head and bring knee back to the chin. Repeat once, relax and do the posture on the other side. Tightens buttocks, stretches neck, legs and abdomen, relaxes the back and spine.

11. A Variation of the Plane Pose. ★★★

(Previously shown in Salute to the Sun.)
Lie down with face to the floor, legs straight behind. Relax. Place your palms flat under your shoulders and invert your toes. Keep your chin on the floor. Now inhale and push your hands so your body rises and rests in a straight position. Arms are now straight. Tuck your tummy in and tense your legs so your buttocks tighten. Breathe out and slowly return to the floor again. This firms the bust, arms, legs and buttocks. It also strengthens the wrists and exercises the toes.

A

B

12. Full Spinal Twist. ★★

This is for advanced students and is a harder version of pose 8. If you have short arms you will find it more difficult. Get into position as pose **8**. Now bend right forward from the lower back, put your left arm under your right knee and try to clasp your hands behind (as in pose **B**). Straighten up and twist around to the right. Now breathe deeply three times and repeat on the other side. An easier version is not to cross your right foot over the left knee.

A

B

13. Modified Version of Headstand. ★★

Kneel on the floor with elbows bent, hands forward. Resting body weight on right leg, keep left knee tight and, dropping the forehead to the floor, sweep leg up at the back. Point toes. Try to get a straight line through the body and don't sway over to the right. Remain in this position, breathing normally, for a few moments.

B. Bend the left knee and take the foot towards your head. Try and raise your left hip for greater stretch. Breathe normally. Return to original position and repeat both postures on the other side. Tipping your body upside down like this gets the circulation going and has a rejuvenating effect. Bending the leg stretches thighs and tightens buttocks at the same time.

14. The Mountain Pose. ★★

With feet 18 inches apart, palms down in front of head (also apart in line with feet) raise buttocks. Keep arms and legs straight, knees tight. Push heels down to the floor. Try to lower head between arms to the floor (our model can't do this). This strengthens wrists and ankles, stretches calves and backs of thighs.

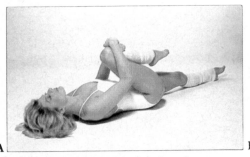

A

B

C

15. Preparation for the Plough and Shoulder Stand. ★

Lie flat on the floor in the corpse pose. Inhaling, raise one leg vertically and bend it to the chest, exhaling. Breathing normally, hold the bent knee and tug towards the chest. Hold pose. Repeat with other leg.

B. Now raise both legs vertically, inhaling, and bend them to the chest exhaling. Breathe normally. Grasp legs in both arms and hug to the chest.

C. Still grasping both knees to chest, inhale and exhale as you raise your forehead to touch your chest. These postures stretch and prepare the neck and spine for the Plough and the Shoulder Stand. They also massage the abdominal area and stretch thighs and buttocks.

16. The Plough. ★★★

If you have back trouble, do not attempt this pose without a qualified teacher present. This should be done to prepare the neck and spine for the Shoulder Stand. Beginners can try this pose with their hands supporting their backs. They should only lower their legs as far back as is comfortable and, if they aren't doing the shoulder stand afterwards, follow the Plough with the Fish (described after the Shoulder Stand).

Lie flat on the floor, palms facing down for support. Raise head, tilt chin forward then drop head back again. This will make the neck more comfortable. Slowly raise your legs to a vertical position, breathing in, then, very slowly take them over towards the floor behind you. Relax in a straight line, breathing out.
B. Breathing normally, take your feet to the floor behind you. Tighten knees and stretch the backs of the legs. Both these poses

massage the neck, abdomen and chest area while stretching the whole spine at the same time.

To return to the original position, press palms down on the floor or in your back for support and gently lower the back and buttocks to the floor. Raise legs to the vertical position and slowly lower the spine and legs to the floor. This also massages the spine and tightens the abdomen.

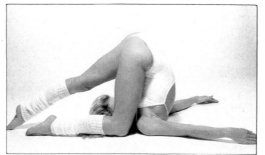
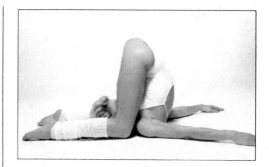

17. The Spider. ★★★

For advanced students only. *On no account to be attempted at home by those with back problems or neck trouble.* Lie flat on the floor, palms pressed down for support, or flat on the back. Raise head, tilt chin forward and lower head. This prepares the back of the neck for the pose. Slowly raise legs vertically and take them back to the floor behind, into the Plough. Now bend the knees either side of head, pressing them against ears.

18. A Variation on The Spider. ★★★

While one knee is on the floor, straighten and stretch back the other leg. Repeat on the other side.
N.B. Remember to do the Fish (described after the Shoulder Stand) after postures such as these which compress the neck area.

19. Variation on The Plough. ★★★

Pressing palms down on the floor for support and breathing normally, stretch legs wide apart and hold. Scissor open and closed, keeping toes on the floor. Good for inner thighs and limbering-up the pelvic area.

20. Variations on The Plough. ★★★

Lying flat on the floor, tummy tucked in, bend knees, inhale and grasp both insteps. Pull bent knees towards your chest keeping legs apart. Exhale. Try to straighten legs **(B)**, keeping

back flat, tummy smooth. Pull up with legs and stretch them towards the head. Breathe normally. Now keep hold of the insteps and pull them towards the floor **(C)** behind your

head. The back automatically rises. Try to gently rock your body backwards and forwards.

A   B   C   D

21. Variation of the Shoulder Stand. ★★★

For advanced students only. *If you have back trouble this should not be attempted without a qualified teacher present.* Lie on your back with arms down to sides, palms flat on floor. Raise head, tilt chin forward and drop head back again. Make sure your body is in a straight line. Pressing down on palms, breathe in and raise both legs vertically. Breathe out.

Now support your back firmly with your hands, breathe in and raise your body into the shoulder stand **(B)**. Breathe out. You should now be supported by your shoulders, elbows, hands and neck. If you can't raise your legs into this pose from a straight position, then bend them first and straighten them up when you are on your shoulders. Breathe normally when holding pose.

To vary this posture, take your feet and legs slowly down behind your head, into the Plough. Move your hands out behind your back, for support, and 'scissor' your legs up and down, keeping the knees tight. **(C)**.

Another variation **(D)** is to support your back with your hands and try to touch the floor behind your head with one toe. Stretch the raised leg back over your buttocks as far as it will go. Repeat with other side. Breathe normally while doing this pose.

The Shoulder Stand should only be attempted when the back is limbered up first. Benefits: revitalises the whole system, notably the head area. Especially benefitted is the pituitary gland which is the control centre of the endocrine system. By pressure in the neck area, the thyroid gland is also massaged. The whole system is refreshed and revitalised. **Not suitable before retiring.**

N.B. The Shoulder Stand should always be followed by **The Fish** *(not illustrated)*. The aim of The Fish is to stretch the neck in the opposite direction after it has been compressed. Slowly lower your back from the Shoulder Stand into the corpse pose. Relax for a few moments. Bend your elbows, place your hands under your back for support and raise your abdomen and chest while keeping the head on the floor. Now take your head backwards until the crown is resting on the floor and your neck is arched. Hold this pose for half the time you maintained the Shoulder Stand. Breathe normally.

A   B   C

22. The Leg Stretch. ★★★

Sit up tall with back straight, abdomen pulled in and legs wide apart. Bend right knee and tuck right foot in to touch the top of the inside left thigh. Rest right hand on right knee. Grasp the left ankle or the inside of the left foot. Keeping legs straight, inhale and try to raise your leg up **(B)** keeping knee tight, back straight. Hold. Exhale. Keeping hold of the left ankle or foot, inhale, raise left leg and take it across to the right **(C)**. Excellent for inner thighs. Repeat on other side.

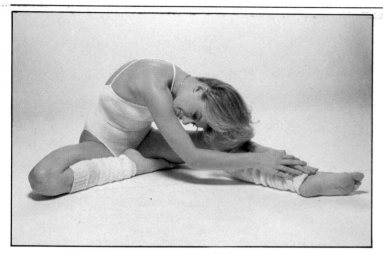

23. Variation on the Forward Bend. ★★

Remain sitting on the floor with legs apart, one leg bent. Face forward, back straight. Inhale, stretch arms to grasp knee or ankle and bend forward from the lower back. Beginners go as far as is comfortable. Advanced students can try to touch their knee with their forehead. Exhale. Relax in pose. Return to upright position and repeat on other side. Stretches lower back and pelvic area.

24. Forward Bend with Side Stretch. ★★

Still in sitting position with legs wide apart, beginners hold left knee or ankle, inhale, and take right arm over the head towards the left knee. Exhale. Look towards the ceiling trying to turn your chest and shoulders up at the same time. Advanced students put elbow on the floor inside the left knee, inhale and reach over to try and grasp the ankle. Relax in pose, breathing normally. Return to upright position and repeat on other side. Stretches waist and insides of thighs.

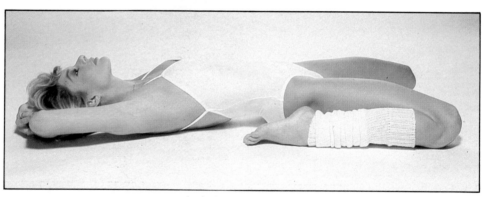

25. The Camel. ★★★

Kneel on the floor with thighs at right-angles to calves. Beginners keep knees a foot apart, invert toes. Advanced students keep knees together and toes flat against the floor. Breathe in and place hands on hips, slightly arching head, neck and back. Breathe out dropping hands to clasp the heels. Push hips forward so spine is fully arched. Hold with normal breathing. This posture opens the chest, stretches the spine and thighs. It is good for hunched shoulders. Beginners may not be able to do the next posture so they can do a Forward Bend. Sit with legs straight out in front and breathe in. Drop head towards knees and, breathing out, stretch arms forward to clasp knees or ankles, bending forward from the lower spine. Try to get your head towards your knees.

26. The Sleeping Thunderbolt. ★★★

Advanced Students can do this straight from The Camel or The Fish. Return to kneeling position, widen feet and sit between them. Some people will find this painful to do and they could put a cushion on the floor between their calves for support. Supporting yourself with your hands on the floor, lie back between your calves. Fold your arms under your neck or head. Relax. This can be a beautifully relaxing posture to stretch the spine, shoulder blades, thighs, knees and ankles.

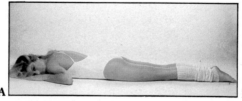

27. The Sphinx. ★

This is a marvellous posture for flexing and strengthening the back and relieving tension in that area. *It is not dangerous for people with back trouble, providing they only go as far as they comfortably can and take things very slowly.*

Lie on your stomach with your face to one side, elbows bent, palms flat on the floor.

Stretching fingers out in front, move palms so they are either side of your forehead. Very slowly lift the head (B) and then raise the back as far as you can. You are now resting on your forearms. Move them for comfort, if necessary. Inhale deeply, expanding the stomach to the floor. Exhale and relax. Very slowly roll the chest back down taking the head to the floor last.

A

B

C

D

28. The Bow. ★★★

For advanced students only. *If you have back problems, consult a qualified teacher before you attempt this.*
Many people find this pose extremely difficult but when you master it, it's very invigorating. The trick is to be relaxed and to

pull hard on the feet rather than trying to strain to lift the thighs. Do not tense the neck area. Lie on stomach, inhale and exhale. Grasp feet or ankles and, in inhalation, raise thighs, head and chest **(B)**. Now try breathing deeply as you automatically rock backwards and forwards **(C)**. Relax to the floor and gently

try to push feet to the floor either side **(D)**. This posture is easier when the knees are apart.

This is a marvellous posture for toning and relaxing the arms, shoulders, back, buttocks, legs and ankles. It relaxes the pelvic area, strengthens the deeper muscles of the back. Now counteract this posture with The Swan.

29. The Swan. ★

This is a very relaxing posture and is often recommended for alleviating insomnia. Try it before retiring. It is a good, effective posture to counteract all backward bends. Kneel with your forehead on the floor and arms stretched in front. You could cross your wrists while keeping palms down.

N.B. To further counteract the backward stretching postures, do a forward bend. Sit with legs straight in front and reach towards

your knees or ankles. Try to rest your forehead on your knees.

A

B

30. Variations on the Swan. ★

Relax on knees and stretch arms out in front. Now take one leg straight back and hold. This limbers up the pelvic area, firms the thighs.

B. Now stiffen your elbows and raise your

head and chest. This puts more pressure on the thighs and buttocks. Relax and repeat both postures on the other side.

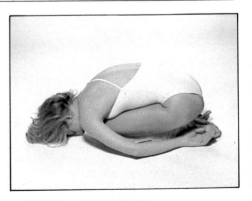

31. The Pose of the Child.

Again this is a very relaxing posture which encourages sleep and counteracts backward bends. Unlike The Swan, hands are flat behind the buttocks or can be clasped at the wrists.

The yoga postures are now complete. Return to the corpse posture and relax!

Pregnancy

Many women think child bearing will spoil their figures and they'll never regain the kind of shape they had before. But the pregnancy experience could actually be turned to their advantage. If you are a little overweight, have got out of condition and into bad eating habits, then pregnancy is an ideal time to start exercising and balancing your weight through a more healthy eating pattern.

Right now we are learning so much about the positive effects of physical movement and healthy eating, we may soon discover that many ailments attributed to the childbirth experience can be lessened or even avoided altogether.

Obviously the strain of carrying a baby puts a lot of pressure on the abdominal muscles, spine and pelvic floor. It makes sense to be in good shape before pregnancy and to strengthen the abdominal muscles in particular.

If you try to get into good shape *before* you become pregnant you will find it much easier to regain your former shape – or even attain a better one, afterwards.

Another sound reason for being in satisfactory physical condition before pregnancy is the fact that your legs will have to carry around so much more weight. For this reason, strong, healthy leg muscles will prove an asset. They'll improve circulation and fight against varicose veins. If you are supple around the hip and pelvic area, then this has to make the actual birth of the child so much easier.

It is possible that women who lament their weight gain and loss of muscle tone after giving birth weren't in good enough shape beforehand and over indulged in foods while carrying the baby because they were "eating for two".

After the birth, restoring your hard-worked body to good condition through sensible exercise is vital and may even help prevent problems with the pelvic floor in later life.

Here are exercises to try both during pregnancy and after the birth. Before attempting them, check with your medical supervisor that you are in good enough physical condition to embark on them.

Pregnancy Exercises

Only do these exercises as far as they are comfortable. On no account strain.

A

B

C

D

E

F

Exercise 1. ★

A. Sit upright with knees apart and soles of feet together. Grasp feet or legs.
B. Stretch neck back and to front again.
C. With hands resting on legs, raise shoulders towards ears.
D. Push shoulders down keeping ribs still.
E. With arms relaxed, stretch neck back again with mouth open.
F. Stretch neck with mouth closed.

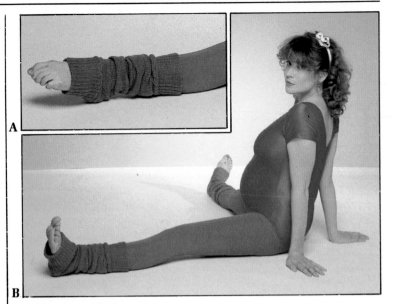

A

B

Exercise 2. ★

A. Sitting with legs in front, place arms on floor for support and point toes.
B. Now flex feet up. Repeat both exercises a few times.

Exercise 3. ★★

A. Open legs wide apart and point feet.
B. Now flex feet up and repeat a few times.

A

B

Exercise 4. ★★

A. Still with legs apart, place arms straight in front on floor and push forward from the pelvis. Point toes.

B. Turn hands to face each other, bend elbows outwards, flex feet and push forward from pelvis.

Exercise 5. ★★

Keeping shoulders and chest open, raise one arm over head and down to meet other hand. *Repeat on other side.*

A

B

C

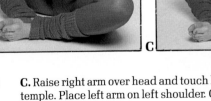

D

Exercise 6. ★

A. With soles together, hands clasped behind head, pull elbows forward.
B. Now try to touch elbows together.

C. Raise right arm over head and touch left temple. Place left arm on left shoulder. Gently pull neck to right.

Repeat on other side.

Exercise 7. ★

A. Sitting cross-legged, raise arms out to shoulder level with palms straight, facing down.

B. Flex hands upwards.
C. Flex hands downwards. Repeat a few times.

Exercise 8. ★★

With legs apart, hands or arms clasped behind back, push forward from pelvis and lightly bounce downwards, flexing then pointing toes.

Exercise 9. ★★

A. Sit with legs crossed. Clasp hands behind back (or hold a handkerchief if your hands don't meet).
Repeat on other side.
B. Raising right arm above head, push right forearm down back from the elbow.
C. Take hands behind back and try to clasp hands in prayer position.
D. Now open out palms.

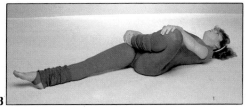

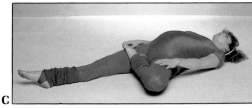

A   B   C

Exercise 10.   ★★

A. Lie flat on floor, spine straight and comfortable with right leg extended. Place arms around left leg and gently pull towards chest.

B. Place left foot on right leg.
C. Gently push knee to floor.
Repeat sequence on other side.

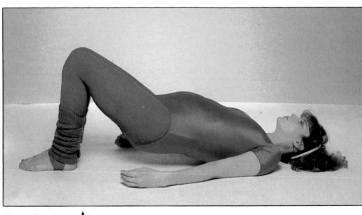

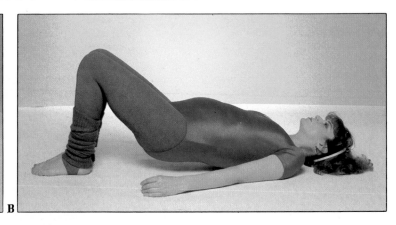

A   B

Exercise 11.   ★

A. With knees bent and hands down to sides for support, gently raise buttocks upwards in small movements. Weight is on shoulders.
B. Lower slightly and repeat.

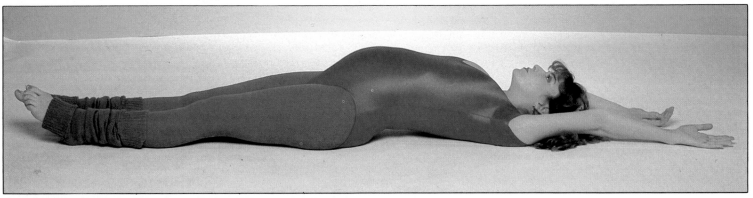

Exercise 12.   ★

Lie flat on floor, feet together, arms above head and stretch out legs and arms.
Relax and repeat.

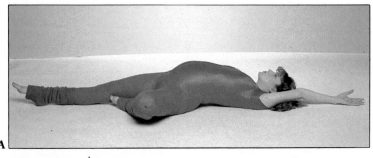

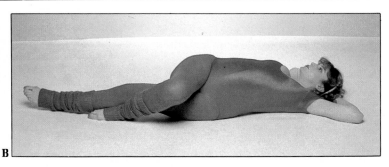

A   B

Exercise 13.   ★

A. Bend left knee outwards and raise left arm above head.
Repeat other side.

B. With hands behind head, shoulders on floor, bend one knee towards chest and take it over body.

Repeat other side.

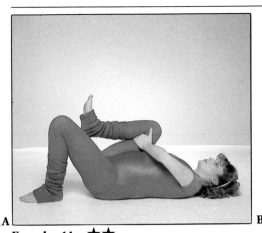

Exercise 14. ★★

A. Lie on floor with both knees bent. Now bend right knee to chest.

B. Now straighten leg and gently pull towards body, pointing foot.

C. Flex foot. Repeat sequence other side.

Exercise 15. ★★

A. Bend knees and pull both legs to chest.
B. Straighten legs as much as possible.

Exercise 16. ★

A. Sit up straight with legs crossed, arms stretched forwards, hands flexed down.
B. Straighten arms above head.

C. Interlock fingers and stretch palms upwards.
D. Keeping arms raised, lean over to the right. And then lean over to the left.

A **B** **C** **D**

Exercise 17. ★

A. Stand up straight, feet slightly apart with elbows together in front. Point finger upwards.
B. Take arms apart.

C. Keeping elbows out at right angles, bring hands together.
D. Open arms out to sides, with palms open, level with shoulders.

A **B** **C** **D**

Exercise 18. ★★

A. Cross arms behind waist and step forward.

B. Bend knee slightly and lean forward.
C. Bend to knee as far as is comfortable.

D. Straighten knee and try to bend to right-angle keeping back straight.

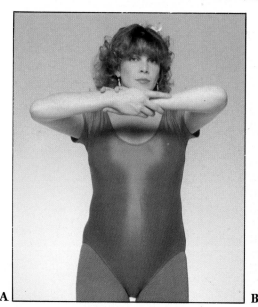
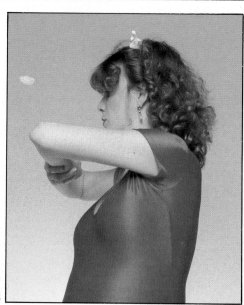

A **B**

Exercise 19. ★

A. Stand with hands clasped in front, elbows out to right-angles.
B. Pull around to one side, then the other.

Exercise 20. ★★

Stand with legs apart. Take left hand as far as it will go towards left foot.
Repeat other side.

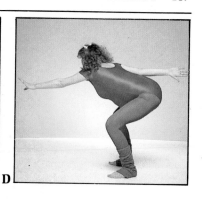

A 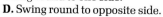 B C D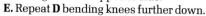

Exercise 21. ★★

A. Stand with feet apart, knees bent and stretch forward keeping back straight.
B. Swing arms to back. Repeat.

C. Extend arms in opposite directions and swing round to one side.
D. Swing round to opposite side.
E. Repeat **D** bending knees further down.

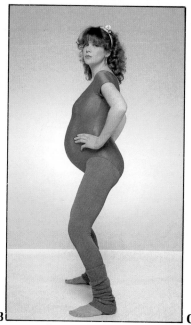

A B C D

Exercise 22. ★

A. With feet apart, knees bent, hands on hips, tilt hips forwards.

B. Tilt hips backwards.
C. Bend hips to one side.

Then repeat other side.

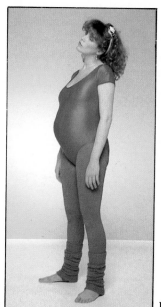
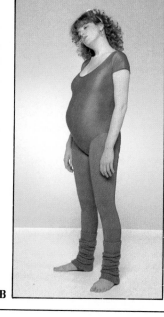

A B

Exercise 23. ★

A. With legs apart, arms down to sides, let neck fall down to side.
Repeat other side.

Exercise 24. ★

Drop forward bending knees and slowly roll back up using the spine.

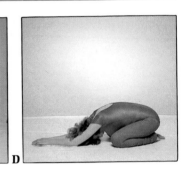

Exercise 25. ★★

A. With feet and hands apart, drop palms to floor. Walk hands back towards feet.
B. Hold position with hands near feet.

C. Straighten back to right-angle and clasp hands behind, arms straight.
D. Bend knees and bring arms to front with elbows bent and palms together.

Exercise 26. ★★★

A. Kneel on floor supported on hands with arms straight, and bring left knee up towards chest.

B. Now take bent knee back and up.
C. Straighten bent leg out behind pushing up. *Return to **A** and repeat sequence.*

D. Bend forward over knees and relax with head down, arms stretched out in front on floor.

Exercise 27. ★★

A. Sit on floor with left foot bent inwards. Take right foot over to outside of left knee. Place left hand on the floor behind. Put right hand on right foot.
B. Change position of arms and pull round to opposite side.

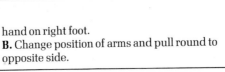

Repeat sequence on other side.

A   B   C   D

Exercise 28. ★★★

A. Squat on floor with feet flat and hands clasped in front.
B. Straighten arms to floor and push forward onto toes, ten times.

C. With feet flat on floor, place hands behind feet.
D. Move hands forward either side of feet and pull head and body towards floor.

  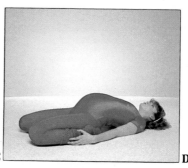 

A   B   C   D

Exercise 29. ★★★

A. Kneel on floor sitting between thighs. If this is not comfortable, just kneel resting on calves. Place hands on floor behind.
B. With weight on hands for support, arch slightly back, bending elbows.

C. Try to go down and lie on the floor with arms to sides.
D. Push back to rest on elbows.
Repeat exercise **B.** Now go back to position **A.**

To wind down. *repeat exercise* **26D.**

Exercise 30. ★

Lie on floor with knees bent to one side. Take arms over head and stretch slightly to toes.
Repeat other side.

Eating for Health

Being in good physical shape means more than just regular exercise. It means taking stock of your whole lifestyle: trying to avoid unnecessarily stressful situations, getting enough sleep, cutting down on smoking and reducing your alcohol intake. But one of the most important things is making sure you are eating enough of the right kind of fibre-rich foods.

The past ten years has seen the blossoming and flourishing of a whole new attitude to food. Suddenly we are really learning the meaning of healthy eating. We are questioning the nutritional value of 'convenience', refined foods and beginning to understand the way fresh and untampered-with foods are so much better for us than those with artificial additives.

We are also understanding the importance of fibre-filled, 'wholefoods' in our daily diet. Wholefoods, as the name implies, are foods which have not been refined, not had anything taken away. As well as being more nutritious than refined or 'convenience' foods, they are more easily digested. These foods include nuts, pulses, brown pasta (made with wholemeal flour) and brown rice, that still has the outside of the grain on. Wholemeal bread should not be confused with some of the other brown-coloured varieties, many of which contain only a percentage of the wholewheat or are even 'browned' with caramel colouring. If you decide to introduce wholefoods into your diet, remember they are more filling than refined foods and you'll need to eat less of them.

It is unnecessary to peel many vegetables such as carrots, turnips, parsnips and potatoes. Many of the vital nutrients lie in the skin or just underneath, so try to scrub them clean instead of peeling (this goes for old potatoes as well as new ones). When vegetables are cooked, they also lose a percentage of their vitamins and minerals in the salted water, so don't cut and soak vegetables hours before they are cooked; try steaming them instead. As well as leafy vegetables such as cabbage and spinach, root varieties also steam successfully.

Compact, metal, collapsible steamers that fit into any size saucepan can be readily bought in hardware shops. They stand on small legs and the water goes underneath leaving the vegetables to cook in the steam on top.

Experiment with vegetarian-style food rather than relying on meat every day. It isn't actually necessary to eat meat more than three times a week as long as you eat sensibly the rest of the time.

Re-Educate Your Eating Habits

If you want to maintain a comfortable weight and remain slim, it is better to work out a sensible eating plan containing nutritious wholefoods, including valuable wholemeal bread and potatoes cooked in their skins, rather than becoming trapped by the 'diet then binge' syndrome. Unfortunately many people are obsessed with dieting. They live on pineapples or hard-boiled eggs for a week, feel totally wrecked after a few days, stuff themselves with cream cakes and chocolate bars, then return to the diet because

they feel guilty. The whole process turns into a never-ending cycle and the fat stays firmly in place.

A fair chunk of the population can't sink their teeth into a buttered currant bun without feeling the deepest pangs of guilt. As a result, the 'forbidden' foods turn into an object of lust and can never be eaten in happy moderation. How can a body be expected to cope with illness if it is constantly subjected to either food lacking in nutrients or hardly any food at all?

A much better plan is to try and re-educate your eating habits for life. Incorporate vitality-inducing, nourishing, fresh foods into your diet, cutting down on sweets, white pastry, fried foods, rich, creamy sauces and fizzy drinks. Instead of eating everything on your plate just because it is there, eat much more slowly and listen to your stomach when it tells you it is full. Then stop eating – even if you've got just one more piece of meat or a single Brussel sprout on your plate. If you don't take any exercise for a few days, then reduce your food intake, otherwise you'll be storing fuel you simply don't need.

If the man sitting opposite you in the restaurant fells trees for a living, chances are he'll *need* a four-course supper. If you sit at a desk all day long and drive the car to the station, you can function perfectly well on one course and some fruit. Never rely on other people's food needs when trying to assess your own.

Foods can be divided into six main groups. These are proteins, fats, carbohydrates, vitamins, minerals and water.

Proteins have many different functions which are vital to health but are especially valuable for building and repairing body tissue. Weight lifters, eager to lose fat and build muscle concentrate on high protein diets. Proteins also help produce energy and assist in the blood clotting process. They are found mainly in meat, poultry and fish, dairy products, nuts and grains.

Fats are another source of energy and help conserve body heat. They also act as vital protective padding for organs. Although fats are a necessary part of diet, too much fat-intake can lead to overweight, heart and circulatory problems.

Carbohydrates provide energy both mental and physical. They also aid the digestive system. Sugars and starches in carbohydrates are converted to glucose which is important for energy. Starch carbohydrates are found in flour, cereals and rice.

Flush Out Your System

Because of the huge variety of soft, bottled and canned drinks available, many people have got completely out of the habit of drinking plain, unadulterated tap water. From a very early age, young children become accustomed to drinking sweetened fluids and fizzy concoctions. Consequently, their craving for sweet things is encouraged (leading to rotting teeth) and natural water tastes dull and unattractive by comparison. This is a great shame since drinking plenty of water each day is tremendously beneficial to the body.

It surprises people to discover they are actually made up of between 60% and 70% water. Roughly half a litre of fluid is lost each day through natural processes such as urinating and sweating. Obviously this needs to be replaced–and preferably not by sweetened drinks containing chemical additives. But as well as replacing lost fluid, water is excellent for flushing out the system, carrying away all the toxic waste leading to a healthier system and a clearer skin.

The experts recommend drinking between three and four pints of water a day. This is a lot for most people to cope with but a daily pint of water is certainly better than none at all. It is much easier to consume large quantities of water if you keep a glass by your side and sip it rather than trying to drink huge glassfuls in one go. You'll be surprised how many glasses you can get through in this way!

It is currently fashionable to drink the bottled varieties of spring water that are readily available in supermarkets and shops up and down the country. Many of these contain minerals which are very important for good health. Others are just simple spring water containing few or no minerals at all . So be sure you read the label on the bottle if you want to know exactly what you are buying–especially since some of the brands are highly priced! For economy purposes, get your daily water intake straight from the tap.

Vitamins for Vitality

Suddenly vitamins are fashionable. They spell not only healthy bodies but clear skin, gleaming hair and strong nails. Health food shops are doing a roaring trade in vitamin pills and these days many women study the labels and make their purchases with the kind of interest they would have formerly reserved for cosmetics counters.

This kind of interest is certainly a welcome one. But if you have a healthy diet that is low in refined or processed foods and full of fresh salads, fruit, vegetables, fresh meat and fish, then extra vitamins won't be a real necessity. Since vitamins and minerals work in harmony with each other, taking large quantities of just one kind could lead to deficiencies in others. So before 'popping' them with abandon, make sure you really need them. Only if you have a serious deficiency should regular vitamin supplements become a part of your health programme.

It is also a mistake to regard vitamin supplements as a panacea for all ills. If you keep late nights, smoke a lot, drink fairly heavily and rely on convenience foods, then taking pills will not make up for the lack of nutrition elsewhere. But when incorporated into a lifestyle that includes regular exercise, lack of stress and sensible eating, vitamins will help build and maintain an efficiently working body that is strong enough to cope more effectively with ailments than a weak and undernourished body.

Vitamins fall into two groups: those that are stored in the body's fat tissues to be used as needed and water soluble ones which need to be replaced each day. Here are the most common ones, what they do and some of the food sources they can be found in.

Vitamin A helps growth, eyesight, good skin and healthy nerve tissues. *Sources: dairy foods, fish oils, kidney, liver, yellow fruits and carrots.*

Vitamin B1 helps convert carbohydrates into energy and build healthy nerves and muscles. *Sources: wholegrains, wheatgerm, nuts, yeast, seafood and green vegetables.*

Vitamin B2 is essential for growth, the health of the mouth, hair and eyesight. *Sources: soya beans, yeast, eggs, nuts, milk and cheese.*

Vitamin B3 is good for digestion, nerve function and healthy skin. *Sources: chicken, wholegrains, kidneys, fish, pulses.*

Vitamin B5 assists in the correct use of foods, tissue growth and balancing the adrenal gland. *Sources: yeast, wholegrains, nuts, liver, eggs.*

Vitamin B6 helps the body's use of protein, builds nerves and muscles and encourages correct development of red blood cells. *Sources: wholegrains, cabbage, milk, bananas, poultry, mackerel and vegetables.*

Vitamin B12 aids health of nerves, the body's use of protein and is essential for correct function of body cells. *Sources: cheese, milk, soya beans, eggs, poultry and fish.*

Biotin promotes healthy skin, helps form fatty acids and balances nerves. *Sources: blackcurrants, liver, kidney, vegetables, cheese, nuts.*

Folic Acid is essential for growth, correct blood formation and aids fertility. *Sources: offal meats, yeast, raw cabbage, watercress, green vegetables.*

Vitamin C helps heal wounds, aids skin formation, makes for healthy gums, teeth and bones. *Sources: watercress, cabbage, Brussels sprouts, green peppers, citrus fruit.*

Vitamin D is vital for bone and teeth formation and assists the body's use of calcium. *Sources: fish oils, butter, eggs, margarine, sunshine.*

Vitamin E normalises metabolism, aids fertility. *Sources: oils, green vegetables, carrots, cheese, wholegrains, egg yolk.*

Vitamin K aids the blood clotting process. *Sources: liver, potatoes, wholegrains, green vegetables, oils.*

Mineral Power

One of the most fascinating areas of nutrition right now is minerals. Most people are pretty aware of the importance of vitamins but few understand the true value of minerals–including nutrition experts who are currently researching this intriguing area. But what is becoming clear is that minerals are vitally important to our well being and have tremendous power over our health–in both a positive and a negative way.

We have approximately 80 minerals naturally present in our bodies–including gold and silver in minute amounts. Then, of course, there are the well-known ones like calcium, magnesium and potassium.

Recent research into minerals is uncovering some startling facts. For example, mineral deficiencies are linked with a whole host of

nervous disorders, organ malfunctions and are even associated with early ageing and cancer.

Another interesting point is the fact they can sometimes act in two ways. Take copper, for instance, which is found in shellfish, some green vegetables, whole cereals and organ meats, among other things. While copper is known to be beneficial in small amounts – copper deficiencies are associated with hair loss, anaemia and skin sores – high levels of copper are thought to be harmful to our health, contributing to kidney disease and hardening of the arteries.

A further example of this somewhat schizophrenic action can be found in sodium. Although sodium has its useful role to play in the correct functioning of our bodies, too much of it leads to fluid retention and high blood pressure. Sodium is found in salt and many of us consume far more salt than is necessary, without realising it. Apart from the fact most people already add salt to cooked food, it is also found in a huge variety of ready-prepared and processed foods. Just try reading the labels on the cans and packets in supermarkets to see exactly how much salt we could be consuming each day!

Some minerals are known to have a positively bad effect on our health and these are known as toxic minerals. Cadmium, which is found in some refined and canned foods plus detergents and fertilisers, leads to hypertension and kidney or liver damage, among other things. Cadmium can also be stored in the body for a number of years.

Lead is the subject of much controversy right now since many people consider it to cause behaviour problems, particularly in children. Lead is pumped into the atmosphere through car exhaust fumes and there is currently a campaign to ban lead from petrol. Positive effects of lead are unknown. Bad effects include depression, nausea, digestive disorders and insomnia. A huge excess can kill.

Some minerals have been found actually to aid the work of the vitamins present in our bodies. For example, vitamin B6, which is now thought to help prevent disorders such as pre-menstrual tension, is hindered in its task if the mineral zinc is deficient.

What is clear about minerals is that they play an integral part in the correct functioning of the body and that they seem to work properly when they are present in the right amount. As with vitamins, many minerals are lost in the food refining process which supports the case for eating as many pure, unrefined foods in the daily diet as possible.

Nutritional minerals include **calcium** which is found in fresh vegetables, nuts, wholeoats and dairy foods. Calcium is necessary for healthy bones, teeth and nails. It also helps develop muscle power and plays a small part in correctly balancing the nerves. **Magnesium** is needed for producing energy and regulating the nervous system. Lack of it can lead to depression and irritability

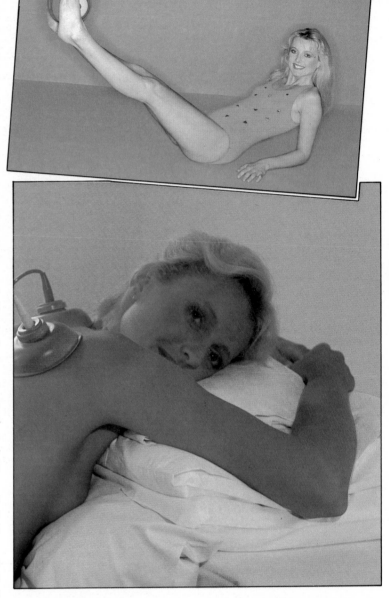

and is linked with premature ageing. It is found in nuts, wholegrains, sesame seeds and some green, leafy vegetables. **Iron** which is found in liver, egg yolk, yeast, wholegrains and dried apricots is associated with anaemia, fatigue, poor memory and thin nails when there is a deficiency. **Manganese** helps balance blood sugar levels and assists in the functioning of the pituitary and thyroid glands. Deficiency is thought to lead to poor fertility and loss of sexual drive. Pineapples, bran, kelp (which comes from the sea), beans, peas and green leafy vegetables are rich sources of manganese.

First English edition published by Colour Library Books Ltd.
© 1983 Illustrations and text: Colour Library International Ltd.
   99 Park Avenue, New York, N.Y. 10016, U.S.A.
This edition published by Greenwich House, a division of Arlington House, Inc., distributed by Crown Publishers, Inc.
h g f e d c b a
Color separations by Reprocolor Llovet, Barcelona, Spain.
Printed and bound in Barcelona, Spain, by Edigraf and Eurobinder.
ISBN 0-517-428628